*W*omen *A*stronauts

A B O A R D T H E
S H U T T L E

Mary Virginia Fox

Julian Messner New York
A DIVISION OF SIMON & SCHUSTER INC.

Revised Julian Messner Edition, 1987
Published by Julian Messner
A Division of Simon & Schuster Inc.
Simon & Schuster Building
Rockefeller Center
1230 Avenue of the Americas
New York, NY 10020
All photos courtesy of NASA
JULIAN MESSNER and colophon are trademarks
of Simon & Schuster Inc.

Designed by G. Laurens
Manufactured in the United States of America

10 9 8 7 6 5 4 3 2
10 9 8 7 6 5 4 3 2 1 (pbk.)

Library of Congress Cataloging in Publication Data

Fox, Mary Virginia.
Women astronauts aboard the shuttle.

Bibliography: p. 130
Includes index.
Summary: Describes the June, 1983, flight of the space
shuttle with emphasis on the experiences of Sally Ride,
the first American woman to fly in space. Also includes
brief biographies of the eight women astronauts, discus-
sing their training and their future participation in
space flights, and describes recent women recruits and
death of Christa McAuliffe in the 1986 shuttle disaster.
    1. Astronauts—United States—Biography—Juvenile
literature. 2. Women astronauts—United States—
Biography—Juvenile literature. [1. Space shuttles.
    2. Women astronauts] I. Title.
TL789.85.A1F68   1987   629.45'0092'2 [B]   87-10814

ISBN 0-671-64840-3
ISBN 0-671-64841-1 (pbk.)

CONTENTS

INTRODUCTION

On October 4, 1957, the Soviet Union put the first man-made object, called Sputnik, into space. It was no more than a 30-pound ball filled with earth-viewing instruments, yet it was a first timid step toward tearing ourselves away from the shackles of earth's gravity.

The United States was already planning its own journeys into the unknown blackness of space. Satellites loaded with measuring devices and, later, a live monkey were sent aloft before humans made the trip. Finally, in 1961, Alan Shepard was sent into space for a trip that lasted only fifteen minutes. In the same year President John F. Kennedy made an almost unbelievable pledge: that within a decade an American astronaut would land on the moon and return safely.

That goal was accomplished with the greatest technical mobilization the world had known. The cost was $25 billion—considerably more than Orville and Wilbur Wright had spent sixty-six years before to write the first chapter of aviation history with a flight that measured just 120 feet!

Even though the United States dazzled the world with dramatic accomplishments, some critics complained that moon rocks were not a profitable product. Scientists, in turn, pointed out that much of our high-tech industry on earth owed a real debt to the space research program.

To make even greater use of space travel, the United States developed Skylab. This 48-foot-long, 80,000-pound workshop soared into orbit atop a three-stage rocket as tall as a thirty-six-story building. Scientists were elated with the information beamed back to earth, but still critics complained about the cost of the project.

There was no way to keep this valuable piece of equipment in permanent orbit, and throw-away rockets didn't set too well with budget-conscious Congress. Thus the shuttle was conceived as a reusable vehicle that could launch more than one satellite per mission, and that might ultimately be used for commercial projects as well as military surveillance. A very ambitious schedule of launches was planned.

New personnel had to be trained to handle all the future shuttle missions. No longer would astronauts have to be military-trained pilots. Scientists would be monitoring the experiments to be sent into space, and there was no reason that women should not make up part of this new breed of space traveler. NASA was looking for men and women who were not only brilliant in their own fields, but who were also able to stretch their horizons to cover a myriad of scientific problems. This book tells of the first American women to fly in space. All eight proved to be courageous, hardworking, brilliant, and respected crew members.

Suddenly, on January 28, 1986, the shuttle program came to an agonizing halt. With the explosion of *Challenger* high above the Atlantic Ocean, what had seemed to be routine "bus-schedule trips" into space were suddenly recognized as highly complicated, risky ventures into the unknown. Two women, Judith Resnik, an astronaut, and Christa McAuliffe, a teacher and the first civilian to enter the space program, were among the seven crew members who died in the disaster. Equipment would have to be redesigned. Judgment procedures would have to be rethought. Priorities would have to be reevaluated. It would take well over a year before a limited shuttle program could be reactivated, but time, thought, and money are putting our plans for a future in space back on track.

It is not the same generous monetary commitment that went into the moon landing venture, but the United States and the world are still seeking answers that can only come from outside our own small planet Earth. Within the next decade a permanent space platform will be built and staffed by astronauts who are now in training.

The first flights of the redesigned shuttle will be for military purposes, but scientific research programs will not be neglected. NASA does not plan to send civilians into space again until confidence in the program has been proved valid. The risks will always be great, but professional astronauts who have been trained to recognize and deal with emergencies will always be needed. Women will continue to be part of our space program in the future.

Kathryn Sullivan remembers that she was seven years old when Neil Armstrong and Edwin Aldrin landed on the moon. From that day on, she says, she hoped to be part of the space program. She hopes that seven-year-olds today will feel the same excitement and wonder in the future of space travel and exploration. Dreams of the future cannot be smothered.

Women like Sally Ride, the first American woman in space, have shown what valuable contributions they can make and surely will be making in our future space plans.

one

Lift-Off

*J*une 18, 1983.

There were knocks on five very important doors at the Cape in Florida that morning. It was time to eat breakfast, not that appetites always correspond to schedules, but it would be the last time for at least six days that shuttle commander Robert Crippen, pilot Rick Hauck, mission specialists John Fabian and Sally Ride, and medical doctor Norman Thagard would be able to enjoy earthly food.

The press had been alerted. The breakfast hour was not to be a private affair. Every bite was to be recorded on film. It was noted that all five astronauts wore matching navy and white T-shirts. The public wanted to know all the details.

Again Sally Ride was the center of attention. She was tanned and curly-haired, with an excited grin, but undoubtedly she was wishing this tedious hour with the press was over so that the important business of the day could begin.

As the first American woman in space, Sally Ride found that her life had suddenly become public property. She

1

Sally Ride and the crew of flight STS-7 speaking to the press at the Kennedy Space Center a few days before the launch.

pointed out that in the past twenty-two years, fifty-seven men had traveled in outer space, but no one listened.

"It may be too bad that our society isn't further along and that this is such a big deal," she said. But it was a big deal, and she carried an added load of responsibility. How she handled herself would affect the future of the other seven women astronauts who were then in training.

She got through the breakfast hour admirably. Now it was time for one last perfunctory check of blood pressure and pulse by a NASA nurse. Then a change of clothing to the blue pants and jacket with the STS-7 (Space Transportation System—Flight Seven) patch, designed especially for this flight, on the pocket. No clumsy pressurized suits for this crew, except during space walks.

Pleats have been stitched into the uniforms with elasticized thread to accommodate the changing dimensions and posture of the astronauts during flight. In near-zero gravity they will grow an inch or two because the disks between the vertebrae of their backs will no longer be pushed down by gravity. Fluids in the lower parts of their bodies will flow upward. Waists will soon be smaller, legs skinnier. All of this will only be temporary.

Now the astronauts are ready to be bused to the launchpad. Already the "hand-over" team has been aboard the shuttle. This is the group of technicians who have spent the last day and a half checking every system, every gauge, every computer to make sure everything is in order. Nothing is left to chance or to one person.

Exactly two hours before the scheduled lift-off time of 7:33 A.M. eastern standard time, the official astronaut van arrives at the base of the launch pad. It is still a gray dawn, but floodlights illuminate the huge bird, giving it an unearthly glow.

The piece of machinery they are all so familiar with is still an awesome sight. Its tail section in flight is as tall as an eight-story building. Now its nose is pointed toward the sky. The three bell-shaped engines are the most advanced liquid-fuel engines ever build. They have to be powerful to lift 4.4 million pounds into space.

The shuttle's stubby wings are swept far back from the cockpit. Two long pencil-shaped rockets on either side of the craft provide most of the power to lift the shuttle off the pad and propel it during the first two minutes of flight. When their job is done, the rockets descend by parachute and are later retrieved by salvage ships.

Only the big belly tank will burn up in the atmosphere after it is empty. The tank is a raw amber color. Someone reasoned correctly that it was just a waste of money to paint it a sparkling white to match the rest of the craft, and that paint would have added an unnecessary 600 pounds of weight.

The astronauts enter an elevator, which takes them up the 374-foot scaffold, or gantry, that holds the shuttle in its launch position. This is their closest look at the strange jigsaw-puzzle surface of the craft that will be their home for the next six days. The entire body of the shuttle is covered with porous cinderlike insulation tiles, thirty-two thousand of them, no two exactly alike. The aluminum shell of the spacecraft is constantly flexing and bending so that it could not be coated without seams.

The elevator stops at the cockpit level. The astronauts are greeted by another team of workers who dust off their shoes and help them adjust their Snoopy hats, the familiar helmets with earphones and communication hookup that are worn during lift-off and landing. This is the only part of their gear that makes them look like space-age travelers.

They crawl through a circular hatch only 40 inches in diameter. Actually there are three levels to this forward section. The pilot's and commander's stations are somewhat like the cockpit of a 747 jet airplane. Control panels line the space below and above the windows and the ceiling. The panels are studded with what look like a thousand soda-can openers. Each tab is a switch. Buttons are not used. It is too easy to press a button accidentally by bumping into it when drifting around in zero gravity.

Each switch controls some essential function of the space-craft. A mission specialist must know each one as well as the pilot does. The reason there are so many controls is that there are three for every function. If, for example, an electrical system fails, a second one takes over, and if this, too, should malfunction, there is a third backup system.

The middle deck where they enter is the living section. On the ground, accommodations seem unbelievably crowded,

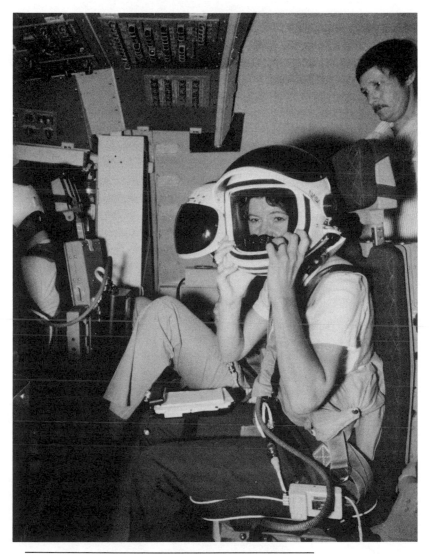

Sally Ride during training for flight STS-7 in the Mission Simulator at the Johnson Space Center.

but after lift-off, that will change. Without gravity, walls and ceilings will become floors. Chairs will be stowed away in the lowest storage section. The astronauts will be able to float easily between decks without a ladder.

Sally Ride crawls forward and up a ladder to her seat behind the pilot. The astronauts settle themselves in their reclining chairs. Actually they are resting on their backs in a seated position with their feet above their heads. This helps them withstand the acceleration during lift-off. Astronauts on earlier flights of Apollo, Gemini, and Mercury rockets had to endure 8.1g of force that jammed their bodies hard against their contoured chairs during blastoff. A "g" is the weight of pull of gravity on the body at sea level. So an 8.1g force would be 8.1 times what you would feel normally.

Sally Ride and her team will be much more comfortable on this flight. They won't feel a pull of more than 3g, just what you might expect while going around a corner in a car at a very fast speed.

They are now strapped in, waiting for that awesome moment. Dr. Ride has been assigned the job of flight engineer. She will be monitoring the workings of the spacecraft. She will be calling them off to the pilot and commander, who in turn are going through their own checklist of measurements. The countdown proceeds exactly on schedule.

Actually the countdown has been going on for almost a year, from the day the crew was announced, and before that, when the purpose of the mission was planned. There have been hours, days, months of drills, and an agonizing wait when *Challenger's* first flight had to be postponed for two months. Their own mission was thus delayed, giving them more time for practice as they went through every phase of the flight.

It had been hard not to go stale, not to let the repetition of the drills keep the crew from being alert for every function they'd now be performing, but they were working for perfection. No one let down.

Everyone is trained to take over all crew members' duties. Even though the mission specialists are not trained as pilots, they have been given enough hours of instruction so that in an emergency they could land the shuttle.

At $T-3.8$ seconds the computers command the three engines to fire. They are more complex than the engines that sent the Apollos to the moon. At this point the spacecraft is operated by computers. Every throttle, every valve is checked and tested fifty times a second. Any abnormality shows up on the flashing control panels in the shuttle and at Mission Control in Houston.

The first engine starts at $T-3.46$ seconds, followed by the other two at 120-millisecond intervals. There is a mighty roar, and the spacecraft shudders for a few seconds, still held down on the launch pad. There is a burst of flame and a billow of steam. Two more seconds and the solid booster power ignites.

Every member of the crew has felt these same sensations in the flight simulators used to train them for this mission, but this is for real.

Lift-off comes at exactly T plus three seconds. The launch tower drops off. As if in slow motion, the rocket gains speed, and the astronauts are shooting through the sky, a trail of white vapor tracking them. There is no time to enjoy the view. Sally Ride is busy keeping an eye on the blinking dials and calling out data on her checklist.

The strongest 3g push comes and goes quickly, two minutes into the flight, just before the solid-fuel rocket boosters have burned off their fuel and dropped by parachute into the ocean. The shuttle is arcing upside down over the ocean. The last acceleration comes five minutes later and lasts a minute. The big belly tank is now empty and drops off.

Two other engines ignite at the rear of the orbiter. They are midgets by comparison, but *Challenger* is now traveling at 17,400 miles per hour. Exactly 8 minutes and 20 seconds after lift-off, *Challenger* is orbiting 184 miles above the earth. Then, 44 minutes and 23.7 seconds after its thunderous launch from Cape Canaveral, the shuttle reaches its final orbiting position beyond the earth's atmosphere.

A NASA spokesman announces on the airwaves, "Space shuttle *Challenger* has delivered to space the largest human payload of all time, four men and one woman." Never before had more than four people been sent aloft at one time. And Sally Ride, at age thirty-two, had made another record as the youngest American astronaut to fly in space.

two

Floating Free

G radually there is a sense of weightlessness. An arm raised to reach forward has a will of its own. It tends to float upward to shoulder height. Suddenly tension eases. Grins appear on all five faces, and a whoop of enthusiasm is beamed down to Houston.

"How is it up there?" mission communicator Roy Bridges asks.

Sally Ride's answer comes back from outer space. "Have you ever been to Disneyland? Well, this is definitely an E ticket." The E ticket was once the premium pass for the spectacular rides.

Commander Crippen, the only crew member who has been up in space before, announces that there is really nothing to report at the moment. Sally Ride interrupts, "I'm not so sure I'd go along with that."

All the astronauts have unbuckled their launch harnesses and removed their helmets. They have been advised to move slowly at first in the unaccustomed weightlessness to

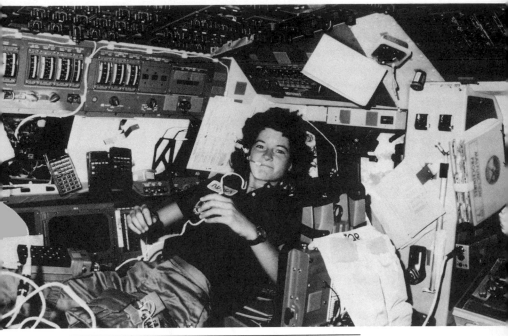

On the flight deck, Sally Ride learns to handle the shuttle's systems and equipment in the weightless conditions of space.

avoid what some space travelers had experienced before, a queasy feeling in the pit of their stomach, known as space-adaption syndrome. Dr. Thagard had been added to the original crew to observe such symptoms, to test the crew's reflexes, and to keep his "patients" physically fit. Some are now testing their space legs by floating around the cabin.

Housekeeping chores come first. Equipment used only during the launch and landing is stowed below. The huge 60-foot-long clamshell-shaped doors of the cargo hold have to be opened immediately to dissipate the heat that builds up inside on lift-off.

Two hours into the mission the first television pictures of the cargo hold are sent down to Houston. The camera moves to give a magnificent view of the earth below: its waters royal blue, its clouds creamy white, its continents beige, red, green, and dark brown, an occasional lake or river glinting silver as the sun strikes at just the right angle.

It's an extraordinarily beautiful picture that no one has really been able to describe in words. The sight of whole continents at a glance tends to make us forget about political borders and strengthens the feeling of unity on earth.

This is a great day for all those who have been working for months to make this flight a reality, from the scientists to the factory workers who helped build the equipment. They all share the thrill of this view from outer space.

The camera next focuses on the shuttle crew. Each one is busy at a particular chore scheduled precisely on their work sheets, but there is still time for a grin at the camera, a wave to the watching world. It is obvious the astronauts are having fun.

Appetites that had been ignored in the early morning hours now demand attention. Everyone is to have a turn at meal preparation.

There have been many improvements in the menu that is offered to space travelers since John Glenn sampled such food twenty-five years ago. One of the most important experiments assigned to Glenn was to eat a meal in zero gravity. Some worried that it would be hard to swallow in weightless space. Could he force the food into his stomach?

Glenn found that eating was easy once the food was in his mouth, but there wasn't much pleasure in the experience. Nourishment was packaged either in toothpaste-type tubes or in bite-size cubes. Crumbs from the cubes caused problems as they floated around the cabin, fouling instruments. A gummy gelatin was used to coat the cubes on later flights.

At first it was thought that food served in a bowl would float away. Then it was discovered that food mixed with heavy sauces and gravies would stay in the dish.

Food is now preserved in several ways. Some items are dehydrated or freeze-dried. Other foods, such as meat, are packed in foil ready to eat. They have been thermo-stabilized. This means they have been heated enough to kill bacteria and prevent spoilage. Bread is treated with radiation to keep it fresh. Only a few snacks, such as nuts, granola bars, and Life-Savers, are eaten in their usual form.

The galley (kitchen area) of the shuttle is a self-contained unit about the size of a food dispenser, the kind where you put your money in a slot and out comes a candy bar or soft drink.

Menus are planned for nutrition, but they are also planned to taste good and to look as attractive as possible. How can gourmet meals be served in space when everyone is busy working on out-of-this-world problems? It's just a matter of planning. Before the flight, meals are cooked and packaged in individual portions. These portions are assembled into meals, wrapped, and packed in pouches. Each pouch is marked by day and meal. The astronauts have to heat some meals and rehydrate others by adding water to the pouch through a hollow needle. When they drink a liquid, they must insert a plastic straw into the container and clamp it on tightly.

Snacks are among the pantry supplies. However, the planned balanced diet furnishes about 3,000 calories a day. Meals have a minimum of roughage and few items that are hard to digest. Seasonings, such as salt and pepper, come in liquid packages. Most food that is seasoned the way the astronauts would enjoy it on Earth tastes very bland in space. This is caused by a certain nasal congestion that is experienced in zero gravity. Taste is related to smell, so spicy condiments are added to improve the food's flavor.

Cutlery, a can opener, and a pair of scissors to open the packets are standard equipment. They are held on the tray with magnets. The tray is fastened to a table the same way.

Four astronauts eat at one time. The fifth crew member stays on the flight deck to monitor the workings of the shuttle.

The first meal for the astronauts is the hardest. They are standing, holding themselves in place with the help of

The crew of flight STS-7 prepare a meal in the *Challenger's* galley.

suction cups on the soles of their slippers. Sitting down in space requires the use of many muscles. Some try it, but soon give up.

They kid one another about their clumsiness, but good manners are a must in zero gravity. When they dip a spoon or fork into a portion of sticky food, the utensil is immediately coated on all sides—nothing drops off. They must scrape the excess on the side of the dish, making sure that it stays there—it is apt to float toward the ceiling or even land on a neighbor's head. One such mishap occurs on this flight, but someone catches the stray food butterfly-net-style with a whoop of laughter.

For dessert someone suggests they open the jar of jelly beans provided by President Reagan. There is a contest to see who can catch them fastest in midair, no hands allowed.

There's a relaxed attitude on Flight 7. Of course, plenty of terse, technical space jargon is bandied back and forth among the astronauts as they go about their tasks, but the humor and kidding help break the tension.

At one point Ride reports that there are "three turkeys and two hams" aboard. This brings on hoots of laughter.

Is it because a woman is aboard, or did Crippen break the mold of the always-serious, stern commander? It is clear to those eavesdropping that everyone is having a ball.

three

Satellite Away

Some of the crew have washed up before the meal—
even though it's pretty hard to get dirty in this
environment. Some may want to use the bathroom.
There's always plenty of water aboard the shuttle because
the spaceship manufactures its own in outer space. The
shuttle's electricity is produced by three fuel cells. Each
has thirty-two plates. When liquid hydrogen is applied to
one side of the plate and liquid oxygen to the other,
electrical power is generated. The by-product of this process is pure, crystal-clear water.

No showers are provided for short missions. Sponge
baths are the order of the day. There is a personal hygiene
station beside the galley. It has a light, a mirror, and a
hand-washing enclosure. Astronauts slide their hands
through flexible cuffs into a spray chamber. Water is forced
in a jet stream into the chamber, then immediately sucked
back into the disposal tank so that droplets won't float
around the cabin.

Every astronaut has a personal hygiene kit. This includes chemically coated washcloths and towels, and small items such as a toothbrush, toothpaste, dental floss, nail clippers, soap, stick deodorant, comb, brush, lip balm, and skin lotion to counteract the dryness of the air aboard the shuttle. Male crew members' kits also contain shaving cream and a safety razor or a wind-up shaver.

Female astronauts will be provided with tampons if their menstrual period occurs during the flight. Even this equipment has been designed for space. Someone made the suggestion that the tampons be strung together like link sausages, so that they wouldn't float around the cabin if one slipped out of its case. Now they come in a chain and can be snipped free when needed.

The bathroom on the shuttle has been made to look as much like home as possible. There's a light over the right shoulder, and the hatch window on the left offers an out-of-this-world view. But there are some drastic differences in the plumbing.

To use the toilet, or WCS (waste collection system), an astronaut enters the compartment, closes the door, and draws the privacy curtains shut. To remain seated an astronaut must insert his or her soft shoes into the toeholds of foot restraints and snap together a seat belt.

To the right of the commode is a handle. When this handle is pushed forward, the toilet gate valve opens. Air is drawn through the toilet by a fan so that any waste material is carried downward, as it would be with gravity, to a chamber below. A set of vanes, called the slinger, in this chamber shreds the solid waste and deposits it in a thin layer on the chemically treated walls of the waste chamber. When the handle is pushed back, the gate closes and the vent valve opens, leaving the chamber in the vacuum of space. This very quickly dries the waste so that it can be sucked into a holding receptable. Liquid waste moves in an air-flow system into a separate tank and is periodically dumped overboard.

There is still one very important job to be done before the astronauts have their first night of sleep in space. *Challenger* is about to launch one of two communication satellites that are almost identical to the two carried on *Columbia*'s fifth mission in November 1982. It is important to perform this maneuver exactly as planned to prove that this expensive spacecraft has a very practical use. NASA is being paid $11 million to launch the satellites.

On *Challenger*'s seventh orbit, mission specialists Fabian and Ride start the countdown. The crew watches tensely through the rear window of the flight deck overlooking the cargo area. First they set Canada's Anik satellite spinning on its turntable at fifty revolutions a minute so that it won't wobble out of orbit when ejected. About twenty minutes later, computers command the clamps to blow, setting the satellite free. A spring gives the final push, sending the five-ton cylinder on its sixty-day climb to a much higher orbit. Inside the cabin, the astronauts feel only a slight nudge.

Under its own power, the satellite is scheduled to reach a height of 22,300 miles above the earth's surface. It will orbit there at precisely the correct speed to remain stationary over a certain point on Earth. Scientists call this a geostationary orbit.

The crew members congratulate themselves on a job well done so far, but they have twenty-one other experiments to attend to and one more satellite to launch. They will be busy tomorrow.

Night comes every ninety minutes on the flight, so they must schedule their sleep by the clock, not by the sun. Four bunks are provided for the crew. A fifth member is

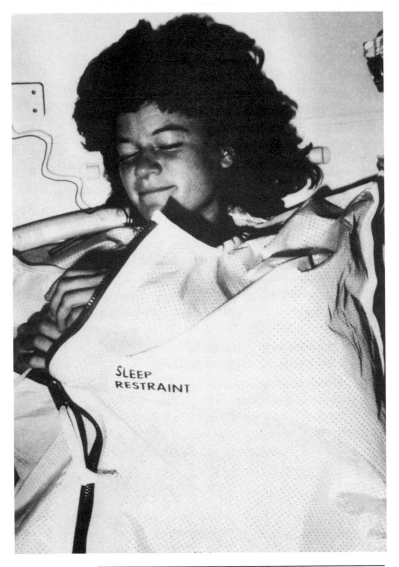

Sally Ride asleep in the shuttle's sleep restraint device.

always alert on the flight deck. Across from the galley is a small alcove with a double-decker bunk. Actually it can provide sleeping room for four persons, because with zero gravity there's no up or down, top or bottom.

The first person floats into the top bunk, the second into the lower bunk. The third sleeper's bed is on the reverse side of the lower bunk and faces the floor. The fourth astronaut is sleeping on his feet, so to speak, as his bunk is set vertically against one end of the two-level bunk.

The beds are padded boards with fireproof sleeping bags attached with just enough pressure to create the illusion of comfortable mattresses. The astronauts slip their arms through straps to keep themselves in place. On earlier missions astronauts slept in tethered sleeping bags without any back support, but their sleep was restless.

Each sleeping space is slightly more than 6 feet long and 30 inches wide. There's a small light and an air-flow duct by each bunk. Eyeshades and earmuffs are available to reduce light and noise, but this is a strange experience, and sleep does not come right away.

Sally Ride tucks herself in, draws a privacy curtain across her small space, and tries not to feel the hum of the spacecraft.

"We Pick Up and Deliver"

*T*he next morning NASA wakes the crew with a "Rise and Shine" program of lively music, although most of them admit that they were awake before the cheery greeting. Sally Ride is the only one not to receive Father's Day greetings from the ground for the "dads on board." The men on the flight have ten children among them.

Each person has a specific routine to follow, but the most important item on the day's agenda is the launching of the second satellite, Palapa B. When aloft it will provide a much needed improvement in television and telephone communication to the more than 13,000 scattered islands of Indonesia.

Once more the signal is given. The drum-shaped satellite swirls out of its launch platform right on schedule.

A picture shows four of the astronauts wearing identical blue T-shirts with white lettering that reads, "TFNG, We

Deliver." They are lined up arm-to-arm, grinning like impish kids. It is explained that TFNG stands for "Thirty-five New Guys," the number recruited for the astronaut class of 1978. Only Crippen, an "old guy" from the class of '69, was not allowed to wear one.

A voice from Houston assures him, "That's all right,

Sally Ride wearing her "Thirty-Five New Guys" shirt during the STS-7 mission.

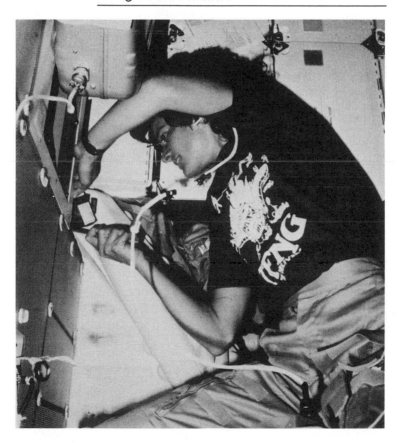

Crip. We can tell you're a steely-eyed veteran from here."

There is little relaxing between chores. Dr. Norm Thagard seems to have the easiest job, because the crew is in top condition. He continues to monitor heartbeat and respiration when the astronauts are at rest and when they perform on a treadmill.

Sally Ride comments, "I'm probably one of the few people ever to run across the Indian Ocean."

There are experiments to activate in the cabin area and by remote control in the payload bay. The seven Getaway Specials, those small cannisters in the cargo hold, are sold by NASA for $3,000 to $10,000. One contains a colony of ants to be observed on TV. How are they affected by zero gravity? Another contains radish seeds to see how plants can tell where to lay down their roots. Another experiment concerns the formation of crystals in microgravity.

The mission specialists are in charge of what might be called our first space factory. In a process known as electrophoresis, electrical fields spearate biological compounds of protein with greater purity than can be accomplished on earth. A representative from the firm of McDonnell Douglas has reported that "Our long-range goal is to install a production unit in some kind of earth-orbiting facility by 1989." The STS-7 crew is helping to set up the prototype.

Plenty of serious work is being done, but the crew members never lose their sense of humor. At the end of the third day the five astronauts and Mission Control do a comic routine from an old television series, *The Waltons*, passing out good-nights to one another, name by name, including "Good night, John Boy."

The broadcast ends with Sally Ride asking, "Who was that masked man?" straight out of *The Lone Ranger*. These exchanges are followed by the recorded sound of crickets chirping.

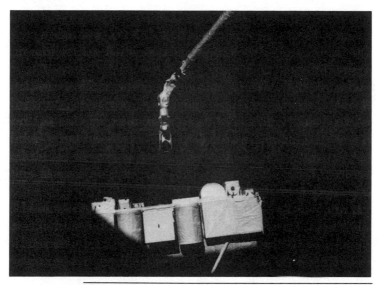

The shuttle's remote manipulator system, or robot arm, in use during flight STS-7 in June, 1983.

The mission's highlight comes on the fifth day. The robot arm in the payload bay is to be used for the first time. Sally Ride has been chosen for the mission partly because she has experience with the remote manipulator system, the RMS. This is a 50-foot-long boom, roughly the diameter of a telephone pole. It is jointed in four places and has a grapple and a television camera at its free end. It can be bent, folded, swiveled, swung, and extended by remote control from the cabin compartment of the shuttle.

The job of the mission specialists is to pick up a 3,300-pound self-contained lab, the West German-built Shuttle Pallet Satellite, or SPAS, and set it adrift outside *Challenger*. The $23 million package carries a remote-controlled television camera and eight experiments. In space those experiments can be conducted with less vibration than aboard the shuttle. This SPAS will monitor the effect of the shuttle on its immediate environment. It will also be retrieved from space, a job that the astronauts must get used to. It will be important in the future in repairing malfunctioning satellites.

Again Sally Ride and John Fabian stand before the computer console on the aft flight deck. Ride calls out commands. Fabian flips switches that activate the huge

Sally Ride and her colleague John Fabian working with the robot arm simulator on the ground before flight STS-7.

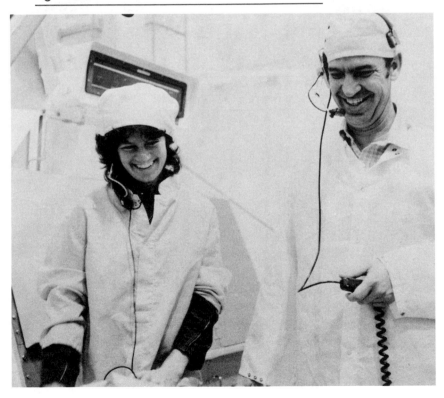

arm. Carefully and in slow motion, a snarelike device at the end of the arm grabs hold of the satellite and lifts it out of the spaceship. Now it floats free, moving at the same speed as the spaceship. Almost immediately, the astronauts snatch it back.

Finding no problems with the RMS, they let the flying lab float free again, and *Challenger* moves away, using its small thruster maneuvering engines. Five times Ride and Fabian retrieve and release the satellite, taking turns at the controls. Dr. Thagard is allowed to work the manipulator on one catch. He is being trained to serve as their backup, if needed.

For the first time, spectacular pictures of the orbiting *Challenger* are shown on the screen, taken from a distance of a thousand feet by the flying lab SPAS.

"Beautiful," exclaims Guy Gardner from Mission Control in Houston.

"You've got five very happy people up here," Astronaut Rick Hauck says.

"There are several thousand happy people down here," Gardner replies.

The SPAS is finally tucked away in the cargo hold to be used on another mission.

When all is secured, Crippen announces proudly, "We've been told some crews in the past have claimed, 'We deliver,' Well, for Flight Seven, 'We pick up and deliver.' "

So far everything has been on schedule, just the way the crew practiced the mission. In space talk, there have been far fewer anomalies than on any previous flight—an anomaly being a glitch, a screw-up, or an unexpected malfunction of some system.

It isn't until the fifth day in orbit that the crew learns of a big glitch—one that they can't control: storm clouds are hugging the Florida coast.

five

Weather Glitch

STS-7 was scheduled to be the first shuttle flight to land on the runway adjacent to Cape Canaveral. A new three-mile landing strip had been prepared. This was where pilots Crippen and Hauck had been practicing touchdowns.

Nothing is ever planned on a space mission without a contingency procedure. If a Florida landing definitely had to be canceled, the crew would head for a dry lake bed in the Mojave Desert in California. All other shuttle flights had used this huge, natural flat land that allowed for plenty of space for landing. If the original plans had to be scrapped, however, the crew would be disappointed.

Using the Florida landing site would save money and time in readying the _Challenger_ for its next mission. If the shuttle landed in California, it would have to be flown piggyback to the Cape for its next launch. Precious days would be lost from a tight schedule, and the flight would drain money from an already tight budget.

Besides, the press, visiting dignitaries, and the President of the United States are planning to greet *Challenger* when it arrives on the East Coast. The choice of a landing site is a difficult one. Consultations flash back and forth through the airwaves.

At first it seems best to delay the landing until the Florida weather clears. The astronauts cheerfully endorse this idea. They say they will gladly stay aloft for a few more swings around their home planet.

Then some quirks develop in the gauges monitoring one of the auxiliary power units that control the steering and braking systems during landing. There will be no problem if the backup units hold, but this is a special flight that affects the entire NASA program, and so no one wants to take any unnecessary risks. Besides, much to the glee of Californians, their weather is more predictable than what can be expected at the Cape.

Finally Lieutenant General James Abrahamson, head of the shuttle program, sends word to the crew that on their next-to-last orbit they are to reprogram their reentry time and start their long glide home to the desert runway at Edwards Air Force Base.

Crippen acknowledges the change of plan with more than a trace of disappointment. "Well, we would like to have gone there [Florida] very much, but if the weather's bad, that's not the right thing to do."

The crew members slip into specially designed leggings, or antigravity pants. The pants are laced with tubing that can be inflated to put pressure on the lower part of the body. On reentry there is a sudden flow of the body fluids to the legs and feet, reducing the blood supply to the head. If this happens too suddenly, it can cause blackouts. The astronauts have all been tested for stronger gs than are expected now, with no ill effects, but the leggings are a safeguard.

The crew once again strap themselves into the contoured seats they used during lift-off. They will feel the pressure of gravity as their ship slams into the earth's atmosphere.

The descent starts when the shuttle is orbiting 200 miles above the ground at a speed of over 17,000 miles per hour. It ends on a runway half a world away with no more fuel left in the tanks to change course in case of an emergency.

Figures have been run through computers. The pilot and crew have gone through the procedure hundreds of times in flight simulators, but still, the astronauts feel anxious when the first small rocket is fired, because they know how precisely every procedure must be carried out.

To prepare for the deorbit burn, as it is called, the pilot first turns the shuttle around so that it is traveling tail first. This permits the rear thruster engines of the orbital maneuvering system (OMS) engines to put on the brakes, so to speak, by giving the shuttle a short blast of pressure in the opposite direction. These small thrusters are fired for two or three minutes. The exact firing time depends on the weight of the shuttle and its payload.

Now the shuttle is turned around once again so that it is flying nose first and nose up, presenting the heavier insulated belly of the craft to the increasingly denser layers of air. About half an hour after the first deorbit burn, the shuttle has descended to an altitude of 400,000 feet. The space vehicle hits molecules of air so fast and so hard that the air cannot effectively get out of the way. There is a transfer of energy to heat, heat that soars to 2,700 degrees Fahrenheit. The porous insulating tiles on the outer surface of the shuttle are the lifesaving protection against this fiery inferno.

The hot air turns to a blazing, electrified gas that envelops the outer shell of the spacecraft and blocks transmission of radio signals. This blackout trajectory lasts several minutes. Everyone at Mission Control waits anxiously. The crew is busy watching numbers flash across computer screens.

A special airplane has been in the air since dawn on a special assignment to take one picture of *Challenger's* descent—not just an ordinary snapshot, but an infrared picture showing the heating of *Challenger's* underbelly. Are there certain hot spots that need improved protection?

This plane is not an agile fighter than can maneuver quickly. Instead, NASA converted a C-141 transport into an airborne observatory. Behind the cockpit a research-quality telescope is mounted. The crewmen hadn't expected to be called into action for the STS-7 landing, but they are ready.

Suddenly, there's a shout in the observatory plane. "The tracker has it." The massive telescope swings into action. Seconds later a hot blur flashes into view and is gone. The shuttle is moving at nearly 16 times the speed of sound and dropping at almost 2 miles per second. The observatory plane comes no closer than 32 miles from the streaking shuttle, but in less than 1/125 of a second its job is completed.

At a lower altitude, two fast chase planes will move in closer to take pictures of the approach and landing.

At 78,000 feet Crippen switches from automatic pilot and takes over control of the wide sweeping turn that will line up his craft with the black painted stripe on a dazzling white patch of packed earth below him. The craft drops out of the sky. It has no power. Its fuel has been used up in its tremendous vault into space. As it enters the earth's atmosphere, its stubby wings must catch the heavier air at just the right angle to buoy it for a perfect on-target landing. There will be no second chances. The pilot can't swoop up and make another pass if calculations are wrong.

Flight STS-7 comes to an end, as the *Challenger* makes a perfect landing at Edwards Air Force Base, California.

The early-morning sun catches the arrow shape of the shuttle high in the sky. Only a small number of people are on hand to see the *Challenger* come in, but they carry some hurriedly made signs, one proclaiming, "Herstory Made Today by Sally Ride."

One last graceful bank over the stark California landscape and the landing gear is locked into place. The shuttle now looks almost like a normal passenger ship approaching the airfield. It is hard to believe that in its 98-orbit flight the shuttle has traveled 2.5 million miles.

It is a perfect landing. Again there are whoops of joy from inside the cabin, whoops sounding vaguely similar to those on the day of the launch.

Crippen radios, "As I said once before, this is a perfect way to come to California."

Back at the Cape, thousands watch on television the sight they had planned to see live. The capcom from Mission Control sends his message, "Congratulations! The good news is that the beer is very, very cold this morning. The bad news is that it is three thousand miles away."

Sally Ride's mother and father are disappointed not to see their daughter immediately. "We live only a hundred miles from the California runway. We could have stayed at home," Joyce Ride says, but she has no other complaints.

President Reagan speaks to the crew on the telephone, congratulating them all, but particularly singling out Sally Ride. He assures her that she was chosen for the mission because "You were the best person for the job." Sally Ride is not a token woman.

Ride sums up the past 146 hours this way: "The thing that I'll remember most about the flight is that it was fun. In fact, I'm sure it was the most fun I will ever have in my life.

But there is more fun ahead for Sally Ride. NASA was even then planning to send her on another space flight.

six

Sally Ride

S ally Ride doesn't consider herself an extraordinary person. She has a knack for turning off the glare of the spotlight.

A *Washington Post* reporter once asked her how she dealt with the nuisance of being a celebrity. She explained that she solved the problem by flipping the "oblivious" switch.

She rarely offers information about herself unless asked, and she's been asked some pretty dumb questions. One reporter queried, "Do you weep when you have a problem?"

She kept her cool by answering, "Why don't you ask Rick that question?" Rick is male crew member Navy Commander Frederick H. Hauck.

Was she going to wear a bra in outer space? "There's no sag in zero g."

Yes, she enjoyed reading science fiction when she was young, but she also liked Nancy Drew.

Sally Ride, photographed during her historic flight as America's first woman astronaut.

No, she is not a health-food nut. She sometimes goes on binges of hamburgers and fries.

On TV Jane Pauley asked whether Dr. Ride thought she'd be watched more closely than the other astronauts because she was a woman. Ride turned the question back to the reporter: "It seems to me I ought to be asking you that question."

Her family has been in the spotlight, too. Her father teaches political science at Santa Monica Community College and is an assistant to the superintendent of the college. Her mother, Joyce, stayed at home with Sally and her sister, Karen, known by her childhood nickname of Bear, when they were growing up. Now her mother teaches English to foreign students and does volunteer work in a women's prison. Bear, two years younger than Sally, is a Presbyterian minister.

Mrs. Ride laughs when asked what she and her husband did to produce such brilliant achievers. "In a way, you could look at it as neglect. Dale and I simply forgot to tell them there were things they couldn't do. But," she adds, "I think if it had occurred to us to tell them, we would have refrained." She taught her daughters to excel, not to conform.

On second thought, there were two activities in Sally's life her mom admits she might have influenced, one in a negative way. She forced Sally to take piano lessons. Sally had no interest in music at the time and regarded the practice sessions as a grind. Her mother's more positive suggestion was that instead of setting her goal to be a member of the Los Angeles Dodgers baseball team, she might like to play tennis.

Sally has always liked sports, even as a freckle-faced little girl who often talked her way into a game of football or baseball with boys if she couldn't round up a game of her own. Her dad remembers that she used to read the sports pages rather than the comics as a kid.

She started playing tennis when she was ten. She was good, and with serious practice she got better. At eleven she was taking lessons from four-time women's champion Alice Marble. She entered tennis tournaments and won, and was nationally ranked when she was in her early teens.

Billie Jean King watched Sally play and suggested she leave school and turn professional. It was a tough decision to make with praise from such a high source, but there were too many other things Sally wanted to learn off the courts.

She's been quoted as saying she decided against becoming a tennis player because her backhand wasn't strong enough. Her sister Bear says that Sally lacks the "killer instinct" for professional sports. A good friend suggests that boredom set in; Sally had other goals to attain.

Boredom was the only stumbling block Sally ever had to conquer in school. She had always been a good student, but if a subject didn't interest her, she'd turn to daydreaming. One teacher saw her as a clock watcher. Sally remembers that the teacher was dull and the class wasn't interesting enough to keep her from doodling and squirming.

When something was fun to learn, Sally couldn't keep her nose out of a book. The year before she started playing tennis her father took a year's leave of absence from his teaching job, and the family traveled through Europe. Sally remembers it was a surprise to her that people all looked the same, even when they spoke different languages. The hotels and the food were different, however, and every day there were new adventures and new sights. It was a wonderful year. When Sally reentered school, she was moved half a grade ahead of her group.

Sally agrees that her parents often let her decide what she wanted to do, but then she adds with a smile, "Once the decision was made, you know, we had to do it. My father made sure I studied and brought home the right kind of grades."

Science was her love in high school. She credits one very remarkable teacher at Westlake High School. Elizabeth Mommaerts taught physiology. Sally remembers it wasn't the subject as much as the scientific method of her approach that stirred interest. "I had never seen logic personified before," said Sally. She remained a close friend of Elizabeth Mommaerts until the teacher's death in 1972. "She was the one person in the world I most wanted to call [after being selected as an astronaut], even more than my parents," Sally says.

In high school she also took chemistry, physics, trigonometry, and calculus, so that when the time came for college science, she was well prepared.

Dr. Ride went to Swarthmore College for one year, then transferred to Stanford University, principally because she wanted to continue playing serious tournament tennis. She played on the Stanford tennis team and was a star rugby player as well. She graduated with distinction from Stanford with a B.S. in physics and a B.A. in English. "I'd been taking all science courses, and I needed some sanity courses," Sally explains. "So I signed up for a course in Shakespeare. I liked it and just kept on taking that sort of thing."

She never got less than a A in an English course. Her roommate, Molly Tyson, now a technical writer for Apple Computer, remembers, "She wrote English papers the way she wrote science papers. She would turn in three pages and that was it. But she would always see to the heart of things. Her style was to quickly think, figure it out, crystallize it. What she said was very convincing, so there was no need to continue."

Sally was also a very resourceful person, Tyson remembers. Sally's car once broke down on a lonely road when the two of them were returning from a vacation weekend. Tyson was sure they'd have to wait until someone came to their rescue. Sally knew enough about what was under the hood of her Toyota to realize that a bit of Scotch tape could repair a leaking radiator hose. After digging around in the trunk of the car she found a saucepan once used on a camping trip and headed down the road to find a water supply.

Tyson laughs when she says it was one of the few times

she ever saw Sally pick up a kitchen pan. "I only lied once," Tyson says, "when questioned by the FBI about Sally's personality traits when they were considering her astronaut application. But I figured that dust and dirty dishes wouldn't accumulate in a space capsule the way they had in our apartment."

It is a trait Sally probably inherited from her nondomestic mother, who puts priorities on intellectual pursuits, not housework.

Molly describes the Ride family as a loving, easygoing family. No one was required to sit at the table for dinner. People ate what they liked, and if it was cheese and crackers and nuts, that was all right, too. Perhaps it is because of her lack of interest in gourmet cooking that Ride declared the dehydrated, thermostabilized space provisions "pretty good," her former roommate adds.

After college graduation, Sally had to decide whether to do her graduate work in science or English. She turned to her first love, science. She had made the right choice at the right time. She chose astronomy as her major and narrowed her interest to X-ray astronomy and free electron lasers. Her study was in the theoretical behavior of free electrons in a magnetic field, an investigation carried out almost in the abstract as sets of equations. Someday this background could lead to the study of ways to transmit power from orbiting space stations to Earth, but she has never set for herself a narrow goal to follow.

Fred Hargadon, dean of admissions at UCLA, says, "She always left a little room in her life for things to happen." Flexibility has been an asset.

Sally Ride heard about the call for scientist astronauts by reading an article in a campus newspaper. She was winding up her doctorate at Stanford and looking for a postdoctoral post in laser physics.

"I don't know why I wanted to do it. I honestly can't tell you what was going through my mind. I only know I was on my way out of the room to apply while I was still reading the notice in the newspaper."

When the call was issued in 1978, NASA was swamped. Of the 8,079 people who had applied, 1,544 were women. Everyone's record was carefully reviewed, and 208 finalists were summoned in groups of 20 to the Johnson Space Center near Houston for interviews.

"Nobody knew what to expect. From what we'd heard and read, we thought they'd put us in centrifuges, dunk us in ice water, hang us by the toes, anything." Instead, the applicants were met by a team of doctors who put them through a strenuous stress test on a treadmill.

"We look for good, overall conditioning, not superhuman strength or endurance," says Dr. Berry, who helped conduct the testing. "We take into account each candidate's weight in relationship to his or her body build. We weren't half as tough on the applicants as they were on themselves. Basically we were observing how their hearts function under conditions of maximum exercise to pick up blood pressure problems or an irregular heartbeat. But no matter what we told them, the applicants figured this must be *the* fitness test. And although this was not an endurance test, they were secretly competing to see who could stay on the treadmill the longest."

This was no problem for Sally, who keeps in shape by playing tennis and jogging five miles a day. A thorough check of her medical history showed she was in top condition.

Each candidate was interviewed by two psychiatrists. "The first guy was what I would have expected," Sally says. "You sat in a big easy chair and made yourself comfortable. He was very warm. 'Tell me about yourself. Do you love your mother? Why do you love her? How does your sister feel about you?' Freudian things, I guess, but I'm not into psychology."

The second psychiatrist played the role of Mr. Bad Guy. He snapped orders like, "Five-seven-four-one-three. Repeat that backwards." She did, and he gave her another set of figures and another and another, until she failed. The questions kept coming with no chance of getting them all

Sally Ride boarding a small training aircraft at Ellington Air Force Base, Texas.

right. Sally began to sense what the psychiatrist was trying to do—put her on edge—but she managed to keep her cool.

Finally, there was an hour-long interview with the ten-member selection committee. Dr. Carolyn Huntoon was the only woman on the board. Sally remembers that the interview was like the orals for her Ph.D., but with one exception: "There was absolutely nothing you could do to prepare for it."

The committee asked her about her hobbies and her childhood. "I don't know why, because they had it all on paper in front of them, but I just told them what they wanted to know. They were very pleasant and courteous, and they said, 'Thank you.' That's all."

It was a long wait to hear the committee's decision. Sally was sure some women would be chosen, but would she be one of them?

"Women in space were inevitable," she says. "At the very least they need us up there for biological experiments. Also, we're part of a change in attitude toward astronauts. We're not godlike, infallible people, but technicians, scientists who will make outer space accessible to the average person and help build space colonies of the future. That's an incredible thing to be part of."

About a month after the interviews, Sally got a call from George Abbey, who is in charge of flight operation, asking if she was still interested. The answer was a resounding "Absolutely."

She immediately called her family. Her mother was just as excited as Sally, but she hadn't lost her sense of humor. "I knew at least one of you girls would get to heaven," she said.

"I think I'll even beat my minister sister," Sally said with a grin.

seven

Judith Resnik

*J*udith Resnik was the second American woman to fly in space and, tragically, the first woman astronaut to die during a mission.

When asked before her first shuttle flight if she wasn't just a little scared, she shook her head and frowned. "No, I'm more curious than apprehensive when it comes to physical challenge."

She wanted to go into space in search of scientific answers. "I don't see myself as having a personal mission. I'm going up there because it's something I enjoy doing, and NASA has some objectives in mind that I can help carry out in a small way. It's my opportunity to do that, and it's a challenge. . . . Progress in science is as exciting to me as sitting in a rocket is to some people. I feel less like Columbus and more like Galileo."

Judy was always a very practical person. She didn't sit around and wait for things to happen to her; she was in the habit of laying out a plan to make sure that they did. Going

Judith Resnik

into astronaut training meant that her life would change
dramatically. She measured the advantages and disadvantages of this new career carefully.

Judy was brought up in Akron, Ohio. Her father was an
optometrist, her mother a legal secretary. She started
school at age four and early on proved to be a very bright
youngster. Her powers of concentration were unusual for a
child of her age.

Other kids on the block were taking piano lessons, but
only Judy applied herself with such diligence that she

became a child prodigy. Judy showed not only talent but also a willingness to spend hours at practice. She continued her musical interest into adulthood and at one time considered a career as a concert pianist.

But like the other woman astronauts, she refused to limit herself to just one interest. Science was her major field, though, even in high school. Judy worked her way through Carnegie-Mellon University in Pittsburgh, graduating in 1970 as an electrical engineer. "I must have been asked a thousand times why a woman would want to be an electrical engineer," she said later. "All I can say is it appealed to me. If I want something, I want it."

She went on to earn her doctorate from the University of Maryland. Her professional honors were impressive. She started designing circuitry for radio control systems for RCA and then worked for a NASA program in which sounding rockets were sent into the high atmosphere to measure temperature, pressure, humidity, and radiation—all very important projects in space research.

She also veered into another field of research as a biomedical engineer at the National Institutes of Health in Bethesda, Maryland, from 1974 to 1977. There she studied the inner workings of the human eye, a subject she'd learned a lot about from her father.

Just before she was selected as an astronaut candidate, Judy was a senior systems engineer in product development with the Xerox Corporation in California. There she not only proved to be a very bright person, but one with determination and a highly developed sense of curiosity. For her, there was always another field of interest to explore. "Becoming an astronaut wasn't a lifelong dream for me, as it was for some people," she admitted candidly. But she felt a job with NASA would further her career, so she went after that job.

From the time Judy heard on a Washington, D.C., talk show that NASA was looking for its first female candidates in space, she wanted the job. To avoid any horrible disappointment, she figured out mathematically her chances of being chosen. She came up with one in five. Then she set about to improve those odds.

To condition herself physically, she started a regular routine of running. Then to make herself more familiar with the aims and history of NASA, she paid frequent visits to the National Air and Space Museum in Washington. She met its director, Apollo astronaut Michael Collins, and explained to him the reason for her intense interest. She was planning to become an astronaut, she told him. Collins wished her well, but he'd heard that speech before. "I talked to my congressman, too," she said, "but for all I knew, NASA was planning to pick names out of a hat." She also started taking flying lessons. She knew she wouldn't be able to match the experience of commercial and military pilots, but she hoped the lessons would give her a slight edge over the other applicants.

Judy was living alone in a Redondo Beach, California, apartment complex when she applied. Her attitude about life was refreshingly straightforward. "I do what I want to do," she said. "I'm single, so I don't have to explain myself to anyone. I'm pretty calm and sort of competitive, too." She prided herself on that independence. "I don't have a lot of friends that I like to call close," she admitted. "I value my privacy and keeping my thoughts to myself."

Yet Judy had an active social life. She was a gourmet cook and enjoyed entertaining small groups.

The day the news came that she had been selected an astronaut candidate, she almost missed it. When her telephone began to ring, she was on her way to work, and the door had closed behind her. She thought twice about returning to answer the phone. But she was glad she did.

She answered the all-important question, "Do you still want the job with NASA?" with a calm affirmative.

When asked later by the press what her first reaction was, her tongue-in-cheek reply was "You could say I was mildly elated." She added that she'd very much like to go up in space right away.

Did she think she and the other women were selected to serve as role models? "No, we might be filling that role inadvertently, but that's not why we were selected. . . . We were first in our fields. We've been 'the only girls on the block,' and you get used to that early," she said.

Being an astronaut did change that nicely planned, very private life of hers, but she felt it was worth it. "I'll keep up with my flying lessons and my scientific studies, no matter what happens."

She was asked what she thought her role in space, specifically as a woman, would be. "We're all astronauts," she answered, annoyed by the amount of attention being given to the women mission specialists. "We'll be going through the same training [as the men]. We'll have the same problems thrown at us, and we'll have to solve them in the same ways. There are no benefits or hardships in being a woman. We're equal in this program."

Judy had developed such a highly disciplined work routine for herself over the years that astronaut training was no hardship. "This is the first semester since I was four that I haven't been in school. I've always worked, so that I never really had a vacation. I've never traveled. I could have gone into space without even having seen California if I hadn't come here for a job."

How did she keep physically fit? she was asked. Did she have any specific training program apart from her running? "No, brute strength and muscle are not a premium in a

Judith Resnik, photographed during her flight aboard the shuttle *Discovery.*

weightless environment—quickness, calmness, and intelligence are. That's what we'll work with. I can't wait."

Judy's ability to stay calm was tested on the first flight of the shuttle *Discovery* in 1984. Just four seconds before the spacecraft's three main engines were to ignite for lift-off, the computer noted that the thrust from one of them was not at the proper level, and the mission was canceled with the chilling warning that the astronauts were to leave the spacecraft immediately. A flicker of flame was causing steam to vent along the side of the booster tanks. There was danger that the fire would spread. Fortunately, it did not. There were moments of alarm, but never panic.

When Judy did get up into space, her main job was to operate the spacecraft's remote control arm and to perform solar power experiments with a 102-foot-high solar sail. On the January 1986 flight she was assigned the job of taking photographs of Halley's Comet, among other things. She was excited about the prospects.

"I think something is only dangerous if you are not prepared for it," she had said of space travel, "or if you don't have control over it, or if you can't think through how to get yourself out of a problem."

On January 28, 1986, Judy was unable to control what happened, but there were those who said she would not have given up the chance of being an astronaut, no matter what the odds. It was a job she loved.

eight

Margaret Rhea Seddon

*M*argaret Rhea Seddon (she is called Rhea, which is pronounced Ray) is a highly trained surgeon. This is one reason she was selected as an astronaut. Dr. Seddon is described as having a glowing personality and an excellent sense of humor. What more could one add to all this? Intelligence and a strong sense of dedication and responsibility.

Rhea is a native of Murfreesboro, Tennessee. Her high school classmates and teachers remember that she had a burning passion to accomplish almost impossible goals. She was a leader, first in line to volunteer for jobs, enthusiastic, and always very efficient.

Rhea's father is a lawyer; her mother was a housewife. Rhea explains, "Mother gave me a love of books and the quiet inward things, and Dad was always encouraging me to try new activities. Once when I was kind of depressed at

Margaret Rhea Seddon, photographed during a meal in orbit.

the University of California, I complained to my father."
Rhea was thinking about going into medicine. Did she
really have the stamina, the background to be successful in
the field? she wondered. Nothing short of being superior
would satisfy her.

She remembers her father's words: "You can go anyplace
in the world if you really want to." It was Rhea who added
the out-of-this-world dimension.

Dr. Seddon graduated from the University of California
in Berkeley in 1970 with a B.S. in physiology. She was
accepted at the University of Tennessee College of Medicine in Memphis. It was close to where she intended to
practice her profession.

She feels strong family ties, not only to this generation,
but to her family roots, her heritage. She is a member of
the National Society of the Daughters of the American
Revolution.

While Rhea was a medical student, she took up flying.
She is a member of the 99's, the International Women
Pilots Association. During every minute she could snatch
from her extremely busy schedule, she was up in the air.
Did she think then that she might someday fly even higher
as an astronaut?

It seemed very improbable, yet she had always been
fascinated by the exploration of space. Her face lights up
with enthusiasm when she talks of colonizing space, not in
the context of science fiction, but in the reality of tomorrow.

"I'd always thought being an astronaut would be a neat
thing to do," she once stated, but she didn't count on it. "I
didn't know if the space program would ever be open to
women," she says. "I decided to become a doctor so that if I
never did get a chance, I would be able to lead a meaningful life."

That meaningful part of her life often stretched into an eighty-hour week. She did regular morning and evening rounds at the hospital, spent hours in surgery and the clinic, and worked every third to fifth day on a twenty-four-hour shift. Her special interest is in the nutritional problems of postoperative patients, or surgical nutrition—"feeding people by vein," she explains.

This is a relatively new field of medicine. Rhea likes to be in on the beginning of new research. She admits that "this specialization made me interesting to the space program. Also, anyone who has an M.D. has a wide scientific background."

When she applied at NASA to become an astronaut, everyone was surprised. Her sister said, "You're crazy. You're willing to pass up $100,000 a year as a surgeon to go into a $22,000-a-year job?"

That salary figure has increased slightly, but Rhea was well aware that she probably had more to lose finacially than any of the other women because of her earning potential as a surgeon. "But this is what I want to do, so I'm going to do it."

Her flying instructor had no idea that Rhea had any ambitions to become an astronaut. "It came as a complete surprise when she asked me to be one of her references."

He remembers her as "a good student, very intelligent, very determined. She did extremely well on the written tests, too, of course, but I'd never really pictured her as a daredevil."

Rhea doesn't think of herself like that either. Being an astronaut was a chance to combine science with an exciting view of the future.

When Dr. Seddon was chosen to come to Houston, she was single and living in an apartment crammed with houseplants. She loves to cook lavish desserts. Does she have a problem with weight? She laughs, "That's a matter between my doctor at NASA and myself." Then she adds, "But I'm a little butterball." At 110 pounds, that's a joke.

When the selection announcement was made, Rhea says, "I was very excited, extremely surprised, knowing the competition, having met some absolutely fantastic people with the interview group I was with. I guess none of us will ever know why some of us were selected and others didn't make it. Everyone seemed eminently qualified." She added, "I guess we are all kind of used to not being ordinary. I notice that the women chosen are all very successful in their fields without being militant women's libbers or overly masculine. We're ladylike—well-mannered, if you like."

Dr. Seddon hopes to examine the effects of space travel on female metabolism. She said, "The myth that women's monthly hormonal cycles make them unfit to be astronauts or presidents will either be proven in space or put to rest. I want to find out the answers to questions. Will women be more emotional than men in space? Can we handle danger?"

Is she frightened? "Personally no, not yet. Professionally, a little. The nightmare is not in dying. It's the thought of not performing well that bothers me."

It is true the sudden attention and publicity have changed her. "I feel the burden to succeed especially because of other women who want to go into the space program. They will be looking to us to do well so that NASA will accept more women in the future."

nine

Shannon Lucid

*T*he story of Shannon Lucid's life reads like an adventure novel with a suspenseful ending to each chapter. When she was only six weeks old, she and her Baptist missionary parents, Oscar and Rachel Wells, were taken prisoner in Shanghai by the invading Japanese army.

Luckily, they were among the first to be released under a prisoner exchange program. Shannon and her parents were able to come back to the United States when she was a year old. The family returned to China after World War II to continue their work, only to be expelled by the Communist government in 1949.

Shannon still remembers some of the highlights of this eventful childhood. One of the most memorable events was bouncing over Chinese mountain passes in a vintage DC-3, looking down on the world below her. She sat with her face pressed against the window, chattering away with all the enthusiasm of a very excited five-year-old. From then on, she dreamed of being a pilot.

53

Shannon Lucid

Space travel was also in her plans. Later, while she was growing up in Bethany, Oklahoma, a suburb of Oklahoma City, she wrote an eighth-grade paper on rocket research. She prefaced her theme with this statement: "If the science shortage is in such dire status as they claim, they'd let women in on the same ground as men."

She set about planning her life to test that claim. After graduating from high school in 1960, Shannon entered Wheaton College in Illinois as a chemistry major. "Wheaton was really a good school," she says, "and I got a good chemistry background there."

Why did she major in chemistry? "When I was in grade school," she remembers, "someone told me that water is composed of hydrogen and oxygen. That seemed to me the most amazing thing, that gases could be liquid. I just couldn't imagine how any human could figure that out. Then someone said that chemists did that sort of thing. So I decided I'd also like to be able to do something like that. They also told me that if you're going to be a chemist, you have to know math. That almost dissuaded me, because I wasn't really good in arithmetic when I was young."

That didn't stop her. It just meant she had to spend a few more hours on that subject, whether she liked it or not. As she began to understand the mystery of figures, she wondered why she had ever hated arithmetic. It has been a good lesson throughout her life. Finding out why she doesn't like something, or even someone, is the first step in making a change.

When Shannon was a student at Wheaton College, she was on a strict budget and had to earn money to pay her living expenses. She worked in the dining room at the student union. Also, a few homeowners in Wheaton, Illinois, were to read about their former cleaning lady in outer space, for that was another job Shannon took on.

"After two years," she says, "I ran out of money. They upped the tuition quite dramatically, and I just couldn't make it."

She transferred to the University of Oklahoma in Norman, which was a less expensive school. She received a B.S. in chemistry in 1963. She still hadn't forgotten her dream of becoming a pilot. She began taking flying lessons, paying for them with odd jobs around the airfield. She could soon count herself a real pro.

Shannon logged more than 2,000 hours of commercial, instrument, and multi-engine flying time, and she wanted to be a commercial pilot in the mid-sixties. She applied for jobs all over the country, but, she says, "I was ten years too early for women in flying. I used to tell myself that I only wanted the job because I was qualified, not because I was a woman." She pauses for a chuckle. "Then, after a while, I began to wonder whether it might not be nice to be somebody's token woman."

That's not the real Lucid talking. She's quick to point out, "I'd rather not be thought of as a woman doing something unusual. I'm just a person doing it."

This is the statement to take seriously, for she never relied on the advantage of being a woman; on the contrary, her career has always been an uphill fight.

After graduation, Shannon spent a year as a teaching assistant at the University of Oklahoma and two years as a senior technician at the Oklahoma Medical Research Foundation. In 1966 she got a job at Kerr-McGee Corporation's technical center in Oklahoma City.

"I did a little bit of everything," she says. "Then I got promoted to the chemistry department and worked with fertilizers."

Ironically, Shannon met her husband, Mike Lucid, when he rejected her for a job there. "I thought she was overqualified," he explains. But he remembered her bright, upbeat outlook on life and her determination to accomplish what she set out to do. Later, when there was a more challenging job opening, she was the first one he called.

He also started calling after working hours. They discovered they shared many interests, and soon they were setting their wedding date. That was in 1967, and a year later their first daughter was born. They named her Kawai.

"In those days they'd only let you work up to seven months when you were having a baby." She was disap-

pointed when someone was trained immediately to take
over her job.

At home she was busy, but she missed the challenge of a
career. Would motherhood put an end to all that? "Mike
suggested I go to graduate school, so I did. I went into
biochemistry because, well, it was offered here, where I
could arrange transportation and baby-sitting."

Another daughter, Shandra, was born in 1970. Shannon
went on to earn a Ph.D. in biochemistry with a minor in
physical chemistry. "It just means that I am looking at the
chemistry of living organisms," she explains.

In 1973 their third child, Michael, was born. Shannon
continued her work at the University of Oklahoma where
she was carrying on research into the effects of carcinogens
on laboratory rats. She remembers life wasn't all that easy,
even with a helpful husband to share the job of raising a
young family. Yet she managed to balance her priorities.
She saved time for family and PTA. It was challenging work
that made the effort worthwhile.

With her degree in hand, she expected to continue her
research and live the ordinary—well, almost ordinary—life
of a suburban housewife. But on the horizon another
challenge presented itself.

"I've always been a space nut," she admits, so when she
heard NASA's call, she longed to reach for the sky. She
talked it over with her family. No one took her too seriously. She was approaching middle age. She had three
children. Her research had nothing to do with outer space,
she thought. But what did she have to lose?

She mailed in her application. She was delightfully
surprised when she made the first cut, and dumbfounded
when the magic word came from George Abbey that she
was one of the chosen six.

Her husband, Mike, was terribly proud. They had already discussed what would happen if she was selected. He'd have to look for a job in Houston if the family was to stay together, but with his technical background he'd have little trouble finding a position.

The older girls were excited about having an astronaut for a mother, but they weren't all that enthusiastic about going to Houston.

"I think moving a few times is good," Shannon explains. "If you get stuck in one place, it's harder to change when you get older."

She was right. The move went smoothly. The family soon settled in and made new friends easily. Shannon herself had the hardest job of adjusting to an entirely new schedule that was rarely on a nine-to-five timetable. There was a certain amount of travel right at the beginning, but everyone pitched in to smooth the way.

Shannon is a special drawing card at the local PTA meetings, although she is extremely modest about her career, honestly surprised she's caused so much notice.

There are times when she gets a bit impatient with reporters who keep asking her how she manages to have a family life with her busy schedule. Her answer is "We do the same work as the men, yet nobody asks them about how their kids feel about their work."

Shannon, the oldest of the women astronauts, was born in 1943—"more mature in a lot of ways than anyone I know," says a friend. "She's a strong person you just turn to naturally for advice. Maybe it's her missionary background, but she can make you feel nothing is unsolvable, and she does it without giving you a sermon."

She's also the tallest of the women, lacking one inch of being a six-footer. She is the first chemist to join the astronaut corps, too.

Shannon's advice for anyone wanting to follow in her

footsteps is to select her own field of interest, preferably science. "Do it well, to the best of your ability. We'll be needing all types of people."

Although Shannon has a strong record of achievement and has never been reticent about shaking up the establishment to make things happen, she is a surprisingly patient, quiet person.

She waited until the spring of 1985 for her first flight in space. "Won't it be great when I'm old and gray to be able to lean back in my rocking chair and remember when I was taking a stroll among the stars," she says. Then, being more practical, she laughs a deep chuckle. "Get to thinking about how your work could benefit from a zero-gravity, high-vacuum environment. Then buy some space on the shuttle and keep my job going."

ten

Kathryn Sullivan

*I*t seems only fitting that Kathryn Sullivan should be the first woman to walk in space. She's been studying satellite maps of the earth ever since they were made available to research scientists. Her own special field is geology, particularly marine geology. Her doctoral thesis concerned the structure and evolution of the continental shelf and deep-sea floor east of the Grand Banks of Newfoundland.

Until space-age scientists learned to track and analyze whole sections of topography from above, our knowledge of underseascapes was limited to figures taken in a painstakingly slow process of recording successive sonar counts. There were other sources of study, too. Sediments from the ocean floor were "mined" and analyzed. Kathy has been involved in all of these, but she kept thinking it would be great fun to float free up there in outer space, looking back at the world she was trying to map and understand.

In her very first interview after having been chosen as an

astronaut candidate, she admitted, "The part I am really looking forward to is the EVA [Extra Vehicular Activity], walking in space. Since I am an earth scientist, the idea of being able to look back at the earth from orbit is truly exciting to me. I'd also love to do more space exploration. I wouldn't mind trying Mars," she added with a laugh. "What a landscape."

Because she is the youngest of the astronauts in training, she may get there. She was twenty-six when she was chosen in 1978.

Kathryn Sullivan

Kathy was born in New Jersey, but her family soon moved to Woodland Hills, California. She is an excellent athlete. Raised as a Christian Scientist, she neither smokes nor drinks.

"I have no special program for staying fit," Kathy admits, "but I'm pretty athletic and basically healthy. I run, play racquet ball, enjoy competitive sailing, and generally stay in motion as much as possible." She's even tried ice hockey.

Had she always dreamed of being an astronaut? "Always," she says very definitely. "At least since the moon landings."

But how did she train for it? Her father, an aeronautical engineer, and her brother, a jet pilot, had more of a shot at it, she thought, so she just continued to do the work she liked best. Her "field assignments," which included research aboard ship, were exciting and actually proved to be very good background for an astronaut.

"I've had experience on board ship working on experiments, which I imagine is not unlike the space shuttle, working at close quarters with people, in isolation," she says. She's had to monitor life-support systems on ship, and she has also been trained in navigation and radio communication. "Being five hundred miles out at sea is very similar to a space mission. You'd better have everything you need and plans for every contingency."

But Kathy laughingly admits things are planned a bit more thoroughly at NASA. "On marine expeditions it was easier to say, 'Throw it aboard; it's close enough; let's go.' Here that freewheeling is not permissible. You work everything out down to the wire. It's a level of discipline I'm striving to improve."

Her training started with an earth science degree from the University of California, Santa Cruz. She spent one year as an undergraduate exchange student at the University of Bergen in Norway. Kathy is a very outgoing person. It's important to her to communicate with people. If it meant learning a new language, she set about doing just that. By the time she graduated from college she had mastered six languages.

"I'd never say 'mastered,'" Kathy corrects, "but I can get by without too much trouble. Some of the Nordic dialects are hard to pronounce, though."

She earned her doctorate in geophysics at Dalhouse University in Halifax, Nova Scotia. She has also taken part in a number of oceanographic expeditions under the auspices of the U.S. Geological Survey and the Woods Hole Oceanographic Institute.

Kathryn Sullivan is no token woman for the astronaut corps, and she hopes that none of her fellow women colleagues are ever accused of such a thing. "I believe NASA chose qualified people," Kathy says. "I wouldn't want to slip in just because I'm a woman. We're putting people's lives, reputations, and a lot of money into hands we'd better trust."

The astronauts themselves are not in the program for the glory or money. Times have changed. There are no lucrative *Life* magazine contracts, no free life insurance packages like the ones that were presented to the original seven astronauts.

"In the early days, NASA was a very new agency," Kathy explains. "No rules were written that governed what an astronaut could or could not accept. This was a whole new ball game. The ball game has subsequently been institutionalized, and we are all now well-trained civil servants. If somebody comes up and offers you a Corvette, unless it's a three-inch plastic model that costs forty-nine cents, you'd better not take it."

In October, 1984, Kathryn Sullivan became the first American woman to make a space walk. Here, she checks equipment in the shuttle's payload bay.

When asked what's important to her about going up in space, she repeats what many other astronauts have said: "It's important for man to have frontiers, to explore and challenge himself. One of the great pluses is that it brings the best people in the world together to break out of formal limitations. The unity it generates is a very good thing."

But she says it didn't really bother her not to be the first woman in space. Having an assignment down the line suits her fine. "Then I'll be less famous and can return to scientific work more quickly."

However that assignment down the line was spectacular enough to bring her all kinds of attention. Kathy was selected as the first woman to walk in space outside the pressurized shuttle environment. In October 1984 she and David Leestma proved that routine repair work could be handled by astronauts suited up in EMU (extravehicular mobility unit) garments.

When not floating around in outer space, Kathy has more close-to-home concerns. A member of the Sierra Club, she is concerned about the earth and oceans she has been studying. "I don't want to be an astronaut just because we mucked up down here and need to run away from the mess. Space exploration works as long as it's not a substitute for taking care of the earth."

Kathy knows she still has a lot of training ahead of her. Even a knowledge of six languages may not be enough. She'll have to learn space talk, that technical, unemotional jargon that communicates all the scientific readouts from space to earth. It may be the most important language of the future.

eleven

Anna Fisher

*A*nna Fisher is described by many of her co-workers as "just a doll." This is not a slur women should take offense at. It means she's a cooperative, friendly, unaffected person who can take on other people's problems as well as her own.

Her good looks have made her one of the photographers' favorites. She has suffered through many an inane interview, fielding silly questions, trying to divert attention to the space research itself.

Anna is very serious about her role for the future. "Mankind needs something to dream about. We've explored our world very thoroughly. The only frontiers left are the ocean and outer space. I want to be a part of that."

Anna decided when she was in the seventh grade that she wanted to be an astronaut. That was when her hero, Commander Alan Shepard, shot into space in his Mercury capsule over the Atlantic. "But it was such a preposterous thought that I could do something like that myself, and I

Anna Fisher

knew people would laugh, so I didn't talk about it."

When she wasn't dreaming of outer space, she practiced ballet and gymnastics. "It's really a great way to help coordination and keep the body flexible," she explains. She had natural talent, but it was the disciplined hours of practice that made her excel in both.

She also found time to enjoy team sports in school. Competition sharpened her desire to win. With three younger brothers, she even managed to be included in games of touch football and softball. Small-boned, almost fragile, she had to rely on her speed and coordination to keep her out of trouble.

Anna has never felt a problem competing with men. She

remembers during medical school "a bunch of us started to play coed water polo. It was fun, because men and women could play with and against each other."

Science was her favorite school subject. Chemistry was her major at UCLA. She chose to go into medicine, she says, "because I thought it would be the best qualification to have if I ever had a chance to be an astronaut."

Anna met her husband, Bill Fisher, while they were medical students. They both specialized in emergency medicine, which takes a cool head and competency in many fields. Her patient load often ran as high as sixty cases a shift.

Bill and Anna Fisher have more than their profession in common. Their free time, whenever they can juggle schedules, is almost always taken up with sports. They are obviously not spectators. "We never watch what we can do."

They play a fiercely competitive game of tennis. They both love skiing and backpacking in the mountains near Los Angeles. Scuba diving is their newest hobby. Anna's eyes light up when she talks about the beauty of undersea life, the thrill and satisfaction of relating to a totally new kind of environment. To her, the rewards of risk-taking always outweigh the potential dangers of the unknown.

Two weeks after Anna and Bill were married, they got wind of NASA's search for qualified astronaut candidates. Both applied. What could they do to prepare themselves?

They believe strongly that running is the most efficient way to improve body conditioning. To psych themselves up, Anna says with a smile, "Bill went out and bought the themes from *Rocky* and *Star Wars* on cassettes. We listened to them and we ran every day."

They worked out as a team, but Anna was the first to be chosen.

"Yes, it was a disappointment for him, but he was very happy for me. I think I was selected first because I had a degree in chemistry before I went into medicine," she says.

Dr. Carolyn Huntoon, a NASA biochemist and a member of the selection panel, agrees. "What we were looking for, first of all, was a strong academic background. But we also searched for people who had taken that background and done something with it. Dr. Fisher diversified. In other words, we wanted someone technically competent, with an advanced degree, and yet someone who could still learn new things."

On their first Christmas in Houston, Bill gave Anna a plaque that read, "The best man for the job may be a woman."

Three years later, Dr. Bill Fisher became an astronaut candidate himself.

"He's always been very proud and supportive," says Anna, "and now it's even better that he has joined the corps. I'm glad I have him to talk everything over with."

With all her accomplishments, Anna admits she tends to depend on her husband in an old-fashioned way. "I don't know if that means I'm weak or just human," she says, "but I need that. I feel very, very lucky to have a husband I love and who loves me, and to be a doctor—and when I think now I'm a astronaut too, it's just incredible. A fairy tale.

"We know we'll always be involved in the space program. We both consider it such an honor and a challenge. I don't think it mattered that much to us who got there first."

Having a family was also an important part of their future plans. Daughter Kirstin Ann was born in 1983. Anna was soon back on her job, but the proud parents are juggling their schedules so there's a parent on hand, and not a babysitter, as much as possible.

Anna sees her job as a special challenge. "There will obviously be a need for men and women trained in emergency medicine. In my lifetime, maybe in the next fifty years, there will be space stations, big ones. Accidents will happen. We'll need to know how to stabilize a patient in zero g environment. It's a whole new area. We have a lot to learn."

twelve

Mary Cleave

*M*ary Cleave—she's tiny and she's impish, taking her job very seriously, but bubbling over with earthy, outrageous humor at any moment.

Part of that humor stems from her job and training as a sanitary engineer. Everybody makes jokes about it, and she does, too, remembering that her mother taught her to read at the age of two while she was sitting on the potty. Ever since, Mary insists she has associated toilet training with higher education.

Mary's mother was a high school biology teacher on Long Island, New York, the third generation of the family to be a naturalist. Mary's father was a trumpet player and conductor.

There was never a great deal of money to indulge three growing daughters, but no one seemed to mind. Mary is the middle child. The Cleaves operated a summer camp on Lake Champlain in the Adirondacks. It was there that Mary saw firsthand what could happen to a crystal-pure body of water polluted by human indifference to the disposal of sewage and industrial waste. Somebody had to care about what was happening. Mary did, but there wasn't much she could do about it then.

Flying—at least, the thought of flying—was a consuming passion of hers at a very early age. By the time she was ten she had assembled every model plane she could get her hands on.

Mary Cleave, in orbit aboard the shuttle

Mary grew up a tomboy, she admits. "My sister says it's a personality type. 'You always have to have one foot over the edge.' I was born that way."

She remembers one Armed Forces Day when her parents took her to an air show at an air force base. She was in heaven. She actually climbed into the cockpit of one of the jets on display. "Boy, I'd like to fly one of these babies," she remembers saying.

She also remembers the answer: "You'll never fly one of these, young lady."

It was a statement she swore she'd prove wrong, but "young ladies" weren't accepted as fighter pilots at the time, and fighting wasn't what Mary wanted to do with that plane, anyway.

By saving every penny she could earn from odd jobs and allowance, and with the generous help of understanding parents, Mary made her dream of flying come true. She had her pilot's license before she was old enough to operate a car.

"I would drive her to the airport in our car," her mother says, "and then she would take me for a ride in the plane." But Mary couldn't tempt many others to fly with her, probably because the sight of the pilot arriving at the field with two pillows under her arm didn't inspire confidence. She sat on one cushion and shoved the other behind her back so she could reach the controls.

If only she could grow faster, she thought. She tried dangling upside down from the top of a door in ski boots, hoping to stretch an inch of growth. Nothing helped. Her adult height is still a diminutive 5 feet 1½ inches, half an inch short even for the airlines' minimum requirements for female flight attendants.

When asked recently if she'd always been interested in space flight, Mary answered with a grin, "Well, one of my favorite books was a novel by Robert Heinlein, entitled *Space Cadet.*"

Yet even though she grew up in a time when rocket travel was described in newspaper headlines as well as in fiction, she never really thought she would have that option. There were plenty of other useful things she wanted to try. She loved the out-of-doors. She was a born naturalist, taking notes, tracking wildlife. Her interests spread to many fields.

"I was just sort of bumping through life," she admits, "like it was bumper cars. You know, just going around aimlessly and then, wham, being spit out over there."

By the time she was eighteen she was desperate for a change of scenery and adventure beyond the home front. Skiing was a favorite sport, and skiing and Colorado went together. She chose to attend Colorado State University.

Mary started out to become a veterinarian. After two years she realized she was just too small to be a large animal vet. Her arms weren't long enough. She switched to biology, intending to be a teacher, like her mother.

Mary seemed to have a way of making life an adventure, even in the not-so-unusual job of teaching. She was hired as a tutor aboard a ship, a "floating campus," where she taught college kids biology as they sailed from port to port. Her interest in ecology and pollution control grew as she saw the devastating effects of civilization around the world. She took samples of water wherever she went and kept records of the analyses.

In 1971, with a definite goal in mind, she entered Utah State University, where she specialized in phycology, the study of algae. "But I gave up telling anyone what I did," she laughs. "They just thought I had a lisp and right away started telling me about their nervous breakdowns."

She worked in the Utah Water Research Laboratory.

Most of the men in the lab were certified engineers. She could see that if she really wanted to have a part in cleaning up the environment, she'd have to get a doctorate in either civil or environmental engineering. She couldn't choose between the two, so she earned both degrees, becoming the first woman to do so at Utah State.

She admits it was an unusual career for a woman. She traveled between labs and sewers. She compares her profession of "sewer worker" to being a mortician. "Such people," she says, "always border on being off-limits to society, and after a while they start to look the part—you know, tattoos, motorcycles, dirty fingernails. They look like they're right out of the fifties."

Mary was the only woman in her inspection crew. She met a wall of resentment. Most of her colleagues had their own views as to what was an appropriate job for a woman.

Mary was not discouraged. She had always been a bit of a maverick. She rode a motorcycle. She dressed in jeans and boots. She was little, but she had a lot of nerve. She could take kidding, and she could dish it right back. She began to be accepted, and her hard work and superior intelligence earned respect.

She first heard about NASA's call for astronaut candidates in 1978 when she was working on her degree. One of her friends handed her an application form, saying she was probably the only engineer in the lab who was crazy enough to try for it.

It sounded like a good idea. Mary felt that someone should start thinking about the future, thinking about how to keep a clean, pure environment for future generations who were bound to start colonizing outer space. We'd done a poor job on earth as we multiplied, Mary told herself. There might be a chance to start space pioneers on the right course. Pioneer—Mary wanted to fit that word.

She filled out all the forms. She was worried that her small physical stature, rather than her academic training, would eliminate her from the competition. But aboard a space vehicle without gravity to require strength, smallness and low body-weight are advantages. She hoped they'd remember that.

Almost by return mail she received a postcard, "Thanks, but no thanks." Polite but final. She had no idea why she had been turned down, but she knew it had been a long shot in the first place.

Mary was delighted, however, that six women were chosen as astronauts. At least they'd broken the sex barrier. Maybe she'd have another chance.

Two years later she did. The call from NASA for applicants was issued again. She filled out the same forms and mailed them.

This time she didn't receive that return postcard. She knew she'd made the first cut because government investigators dropped by her small town of Wellsville, Utah, to make discreet inquiries about the character of one Mary Cleave. Her neighbors couldn't quite figure out why the feds were interested in her.

The next official word was an invitation to come to Houston for interviews. Her surprised fellow workers in the Sanitation Department stopped laughing. Only Mary took it less seriously. At least she'd get a chance to see the Space Center on a special tour. That would be worth the trip. There would be no disappointment, no misty eyes, no matter what the outcome. This was to be a fun experience.

Mary had mixed feelings when she arrived at the NASA complex outside Houston. The stark white concrete buildings with their black-tinted glass windows looked austere, like a college campus without the ivy and without any undergraduates. She could get used to that, but the presence of the military made her uneasy. She was a product of the days of student revolt and antiwar sentiment. "I've always had trouble with authority figures," she admits.

NASA is quick to assert that it is a civilian agency, but most of the male astronauts are high-ranking military officers. Their clothes, even when they were not in uniform, tended to be starched and conservative. Mary wasn't sure that her waist-length hair, corduroys, and earth shoes would quite fit in. She was not one for making changes to fit a mold.

Each group of astronauts went through a series of tests and interviews that lasted from Monday through Friday. A thorough physical came first: blood samples, urine samples, endurance tests; there was no room for health problems in zero gravity.

Then there were lectures on what the work of an astronaut was all about. It was a reverse selling job. Anyone expecting to further a career in a particular field should step back and have second thoughts. "Someone who wants to do research and is doing very well in his field," George Abbey said, "will have to accept the fact that as an astronaut he or she will be implementing someone else's experiments, not his own."

Then there was the scary part of being told all of the things that might happen on a space flight that could bring instant death, or worse. There's no way to parachute out of the space shuttle, and there are only two pressurized space suits on board at any time. If a rescue ship is able to rendezvous with a crippled orbiter, crew members might be transported through the vacuum of space by being tucked into balloons called personal rescue enclosures, fabric spheres 30 inches (76 centimeters) in diameter.

Each applicant was asked to experience a rehearsal of just such a maneuver. Their watches were removed. Then they were told to crawl into an escape ball, which was zipped up after them. They had no idea how long they were expected to stay inside the blackness.

The experiment lasted only fifteen minutes, but some candidates panicked and tried to rip open their balloons. Mary was much smaller than the others and therefore didn't experience quite the same discomfort. She surprised everyone by simply curling up and going to sleep.

Mary still had to meet the two psychiatrists. No one had told her about the Mr. Good Guy–Mr. Bad Guy approach. When she met the gruff, impatient one, she simply called his bluff. "I thought psychiatrists were supposed to be nice and understanding. What's wrong with you?"

She took him so much by surprise that he laughed. He'd met the unflappable candidate. He was more friendly from then on.

One of the questions asked of everyone was "If you were to die and come back as something other than a human, what would that be?"

There were plenty of strange answers, but it took Mary only a moment of thought to answer: "A sea gull, a good practical bird. He cleans up a lot of things. I remember when I was working on a ship, I used to feed them off the fantail."

Another question the committee asked, more out of curiosity than for relevance in selection, was how long each applicant had wanted to be an astronaut.

There were many who answered, "Always," digging up memories from childhood to explain how this dream had dominated their entire lives.

Mary just chuckled. "Are you serious? I'm a pragmatist. I thought you guys would never take women into the program."

Then it was back to Utah. She'd had the grand tour. It

had been fun. She had no expectations that she would be called back, not after meeting so many other great people, all of whom were qualified for those few spots in the elite group of "space cadets."

But the word came on May 28. "Mary, I think we've had enough time to make our decision. If you're still interested, we'd like to have you join us."

Her reply was not "Yes," but rather "Who is this?" She was sure someone was kidding her. When she found out she was talking with George Abbey himself, the excited answer came back loud and clear: "Yes, oh, yes."

Two months later she arrived in Houston for good. It took her three days to drive from Utah, pulling a 24-foot U-Haul trailer. She had been living in a huge old farmhouse with a spectacular view of the mountains. House and view had come with a price tag of $12,500. She wasn't prepared for the Houston shock. The city had been exploding in size, unable to keep pace with the housing demand.

"When I look up I like to see land," Mary said, "but Houston is so flat, you can never see anything except sky. I told my realtor if I couldn't look at mountains I'd have to look at the ocean."

She finally settled for a small cottage set on stilts on the shore of Galveston Bay. It cost her $69,000, but she had sea gulls and herons to keep her company.

During working hours her immediate company consisted of two fellow astronauts, Lieutenant Commander Michael Coats of the navy and Major Richard Mullane of the air force, who were assigned shared duties and a tiny office space. Before she met her colleagues she took a deep breath and crossed her fingers. She'd have to learn to cope with military brass. She didn't know what to expect.

Neither did Coats and Mullane. They agreed to treat their new office-mate just as if she were a plebe. When

Mary walked into her office for the first time, every bit of furniture was stacked on top of her desk, and the desk was shoved behind a bank of filing cabinets.

"Okay, you guys," she said, "you asked for it. The first thing we're going to do is to get rid of this junky government furniture. I'm going to decorate this place in French Provincial. And as soon as you get the floor cleaned up I'm going to put down a mauve rug. Yeah, that'd be nice."

The ice was broken. The only decorating change Mary actually made was to hang her favorite cartoon by Gahan Wilson, showing two characters in gas masks standing in an office. One of them says, "I'm, sorry, Senator. It's some more of those crackpot conservationists." She also put up a picture of her father conducting a symphony orchestra.

Mary was there to stay. NASA would have to cope.

thirteen

Bonnie Dunbar

"**M**ercury, Gemini, Apollo, and Skylab were a Lewis and Clark kind of thing," explains a NASA spokesman. "Now we're sending up settlers. The shuttle is the new Conestoga wagon."

Bonnie Dunbar's parents didn't come to the state of Washington in a covered wagon, but they do fit the picture of pioneers, and they must be just a bit amazed at their daughter's pioneering plans.

"My parents are phenomenal," Bonnie says. "The farm I grew up on in eastern Washington had been barren land until 1948, when my mom and dad homesteaded there. They built a wood-frame tent that my mother lived in most of the time when my dad was doing wheat farming in northern Oregon. . . . There are still tree houses there that I built.

"I was part of the 1949 baby boom that came along some time before Sputnik was launched. I was the oldest of four kids," she explains, "and we were very isolated from the nearest town, so I grew up as a bookworm and lived in an imaginary world. I read a lot of science fiction and a lot of the classics, too."

She feels this rather special upbringing made her self-reliant. Her parents always told her, "Do what you want; if it's really worth it to you, then persevere."

"My folks never steered me," she says, "but they maintained that the only limitations you have are in your mind. We didn't have any college graduates in our family, and because I was the oldest, my mother made me swear I wouldn't get married until I had a college degree. She thought that was important."

Bonnie Dunbar

Bonnie was a good student in both science and literature, but it was a high school physics teacher who encouraged her to major in engineering and to continue reading as a pastime.

"I considered MIT, but it was too expensive, and I also thought of Cal Tech, until someone sent me a very nice letter telling me they didn't have any coeducational dormitories, which was another way of saying that they weren't academically coeducational."

Fate seems to have taken a hand in Bonnie's decision to enroll at the University of Washington. This school had just been commissioned to help develop the heat shield for the space shuttle. Bonnie was in on the earliest research that produced the ceramic tiles that would be used to protect *Columbia* from the temperature extremes of reentry.

People still confuse her technical expertise and her degree as a ceramic engineer with the art of making clay pots. She doesn't bother to tell them her master's thesis was in the field of mechanisms and kinetics of ionic diffusion in sodium beta-alumina.

"I loved science, and I was always interested in the space program," she says. "My generation grew up with space flight as part of the environment. So I could see myself as a jet pilot, a scientist—even flying a spacecraft. I was a bit of a dreamer," she admits. But few people knew she had hopes of traveling in that vehicle she was helping to protect.

"When you go to school and pick out a major, you don't say, 'I'm going to be an astronaut.' The only person I told at that time was the head of the department, because I knew he wouldn't consider me absolutely bonkers."

She can remember sleeping on haystacks at the farm when she was a kid, looking up at the stars and thinking about being "out there."

"I didn't define it as wanting to be an astronaut, but I do remember at one point that I wanted to be a jet pilot. I used to watch the television station sign off at night with a picture of a jet going through the clouds, and I guess I was sort of naive about it. I didn't realize that women weren't jet pilots."

Bonnie didn't wait around idly for NASA to knock on her door. After graduating cum laude from the University of Washington in 1971, she worked for Boeing Computer Services for two years as a systems analyst, then returned to the university to do graduate work in ceramics.

In 1975 she was invited to participate in research at Hartwell Laboratories in Oxford, England. She then accepted a job at Rockwell International, helping to set up production facilities in California for the tiles to be used on the shuttle. She also made some personal contacts at NASA, so she'd be the first to know when they were going to hire new astronauts.

When the call went out in 1978, she was one of the first to apply. She made it through to the finals but was dropped in the last elimination. After that early disappointment, she became more determined than ever to try again.

"In looking over the resumes of those who'd been accepted, I realized that they had a lot of interests and worked in a number of different disciplines," Bonnie said. "I could see that I needed to enlarge my background and improve myself. I was twenty-nine by then, and I was at the point where I didn't want to be known as the tile expert all my life." She set about making a change.

"When I'd been in Houston for interviews for the astronaut program, I'd been offered several jobs at the Johnson Space Center, and I decided there were interesting possibilities in flight operations there. So I went from being a senior research engineer, working in a lab with materials,

Bonnie Dunbar and her colleague Reinhard Furrer work on experiments during shuttle flights STS G1-A.

to being a systems engineer, working in an office with people."

She also represented Rockwell International as a member of the Dr. Kraft Ehricke evaluation committee on ways to use outer space for industrial purposes. It was a way to put her imagination to practical use.

Two years later, when she applied for the astronaut class of 1980, she was accepted. "I just moved my office from one side of the building to another," she says with a laugh.

She hopes that many other women will qualify for space

work. "The reason so few women are selected is that you have to have a science or engineering background. When I started my education, only three percent of the engineering students were women, and now the proportion is up to fifteen or twenty percent. So we're really beginning to see some growth. But I respect NASA for not making the requirements any different for women."

Her conversation often turns to dissipating velocity and synthesizing gravity, but she sprinkles the professional jargon with an occasional "Wow" and "By golly."

That "Wow" is a pretty apt description of what she sees for the future. Bonnie Dunbar claims that the U.S. space program is a tremendous boost for the country's technology and economy.

"As we developed cars, railroads, and airplanes," she points out, "we needed gas stations and air terminals. What we need now is a space station. What we call a space operations center would allow us to do some of the best observations of weather, crops, and oceans, as well as material processing and service repair of vehicles. It's going to happen . . . and it's certainly not going to help us economically to ask either the Japanese or the Europeans to launch our satellites for us."

She also talks about building furnaces in space that could manufacture new alloys and crystals. Bonnie has come a long way from the haystacks, but she's still looking at the stars.

fourteen

*A*stronaut
*C*andidates

*T*urn south from the glass towers of Houston and you'll
be on the freeway heading toward Galveston Bay. You
pass a stretch of used-car lots and bargain warehouse
outlets. It's flat country, and depending on the season, it's
either hot and humid or cold and clammy, just about like a
laundromat, one resident with a sense of humor remarked.
But you're in a neighborhood where some pretty exciting
things happen.

The sign overhead points to the turnoff for the Lyndon
B. Johnson Space Center. It is located in Clear Lake City,
an instant suburb of Houston. Nothing was here twenty-
five years ago.

Before you get to the main gate of the center, you'll see
on your left a very impressive display of obsolete rockets.
Some are pointing toward the sky; others are stretched out

on the ground as if aimed for the highway traffic that speeds by a few hundred feet away.

The firing mechanisms of the space vehicles are monstrously large, but the capsules that housed space travelers look like fiendishly contrived tiny torture chambers.

There's more inside the space museum for tourists to see, but the arriving astronaut candidates (that's what they are called for the first year of their training) have had the tour before, and they are ready to report in. All of them admit to a feeling of excitement that they are to be part of this very special world, planning unheard-of-things for the future.

When the first seven male space travelers (they weren't called astronauts in 1959) arrived in Houston, they were already celebrities. Their names were household words. They were officers of an elite military air force, arriving in sleek cars.

Times have changed. The close-knit cadre of test pilots has disappeared, now that having "the right stuff" most probably means being able to solve quadratic equations in their heads. There are still a lot of top-brass military men around, but uniforms are not worn, and there's no snapping to attention.

The members of the new class of 1978 arrive one at a time, some in old cars, a few in shiny recent models, some in taxis. There doesn't seem to be any standard code of appearance, either. The women are strikingly individual. The tallest, a biochemist and mother of three, is 5 feet 11; the shortest, a mere 5 feet 2, weighing in at 98 pounds. The one trait they all share is that they are hard workers and high achievers.

"The most recent astronaut groups are generally fairly quiet, unassuming people," one Johnson Space Center public information officer comments. "Maybe it's just that the whole space program has matured enough so that we can now settle down to the business of space flight."

The space center itself is a group of white concrete and glass buildings scattered over a well-kept campus. This isn't the climate or atmosphere for ivy-clad bell towers. It is better considered a well-designed factory for scientists searching for answers in outer space.

The first job of the astronauts after checking in is to find a place to live, preferably close to the base. Housing has not kept pace with demand. Some of the women are amazed at the price of even a simple home, but no one ever promised them luxury.

Few grumbles are heard, however. They know that if they drop out of the program, there are hundreds of applicants willing to take their place. And it has been made very clear to them that the government has no intention of investing about $10 million in their future if they aren't going to make this their life's work. This is the estimated cost to train and maintain an astronaut during his or her career at NASA.

Although military uniforms long ago disappeared, clothing is provided for the astronauts, with no regulation as to when it has to be worn. There are comfortable collared T-shirts and slacks for both men and women. Fatigues are issued for rougher work, but they are light blue, gray-green, or drab orange. A specifically designed patch designates their rank as astronaut candidate. Plenty of extra pockets and zippered compartments are provided for the instruments and tools they'll need in their work. Finally, they are fitted with the neat pleated suits they will wear aboard the shuttle. The suits are fireproof and adjustable for changes of posture in space.

The candidates wear these outfits for the first picture-taking, and they command plenty of press coverage, principally because this is the first time women have been selected for the job. Each of them poses for a portrait, interviews are video-taped, and then the press is invited to meet the candidates in the public relations building of the space center.

It is a rather small room with a dais at one end. Microphones are placed all along a table. Lights are trained on those being interviewed, for this, too, will be taped. The questions seem endless and repetitious.

NASA tries to cooperate with the news media, yet shield its protégés until they can adjust to their new public role. They are all made to realize that good public relations for the space program will mean more adequate funding for their training. Once the press has had its day, it is time to settle down to more serious business.

George Abbey, who has had the final voice in their selection, gives the candidates a welcoming speech. He repeats what they were told when they first came to the space center, explaining that they all have to be team players: "People set on doing their own thing, no matter how bright, probably won't be happy here."

Next came the assignments. The women have no opportunity to band together. "George Abbey was very careful about that in assigning office space and so on," Sally Ride explained.

Over the next few weeks the women become friends, "but not really close friends," one of them says. Yet there are times when the six of them are brought together for meetings.

"We got together to chat about certain issues that might come up," one female candidate reports. "We decided if there were issues that would have relevance to future women in space, we would discuss them and have a good position on them."

Astronaut candidates during a break in survival training in 1978. From left to right: Sally Ride, Judith Resnik, Anna Fisher, Kathryn Sullivan and Margaret Rhea Seddon.

They could give NASA advice on flight equipment. They suggested two-piece suits, for example. And they requested that skin lotions, makeup, and tampons be added to their personal hygiene kits. They also suggested that bikini underwear be added to the supply of men's boxer shorts.

Most of them were used to working with men, so there was no feeling of awkwardness here at NASA.

Yet some of the men who had been with the program over the years admitted they had doubts at first. "We all wondered what changes it would make and whether or not the women could cut it," said one.

Apollo and Skylab veteran Alan Bean, who was responsible for training when the new candidates first joined the program, was not at all happy with the idea of women astronauts. Later, he changed his mind, however. The women had had more computer training than most of the old-timers. They were used to solving problems from an analytical point of view.

Bean admitted, "At first I imagined they were just individuals trying to do a man's job. I was proven wrong. . . . Females intuitively understand astronaut skills. They perform the mental and physical tasks as well as men."

"We all knew it was coming," said Bob Crippen, pilot of the first shuttle flight. "The only commotion I can remember around here was building a ladies' room into the gym."

The hardest adjustment for some of the women was starting all over to learn the basics in other fields. Engineers were assigned research in physiology. Doctors studied astronomy, and when they were just about feeling competent in one field, their jobs were shuffled.

No one complained, but pilot astronaut Lieutenant Commander Robert "Hoot" Gibson, who later married Dr. Seddon, says, "Rhea gets a little bit frustrated occasionally. She's a very accomplished person in her field. She's done some hard work and put in a lot of years to be a tremendous surgeon, and then we brought her down here and she didn't know anything. I know what it's like because I was an experienced test pilot, and when I came here I didn't know anything about rocket ships. It means starting all over."

fifteen

Simulating the Mission

*T*raining for men and women specialists is the same—
intense. Whether the person is an astronaut candidate
still under evaluation, a member of the astronaut corps
waiting to be assigned a flight, or a crew member of an
upcoming mission, an astronaut is always in training.

The first-year program breaks down into three parts.
The first phase involves about 140 hours of classroom work
covering the spacecraft in general. There are lectures on
the physics of the shuttle. Why, for example, was it designed with such stubby swept-back wings and such a tall
tail section? Any normal aircraft designed to cruise in the
earth's atmosphere with a cushion of air under its wings
would have those wings ripped off in the first fiery minute
of launch. The tail section gives the shuttle stability when
heading toward home.

The development of the heat shield and wing coating is

93

described. Dozens of products were tested for their protective qualities, lightness of weight, and ability to be applied and replaced easily. The astronauts are beginning to realize what a remarkable piece of machinery they will be responsible for and how many people have had a hand in its development.

The power mechanisms of the craft are explained, from the tremendous rocket engines at lift-off to the more moderate thrusters that maneuver the shuttle in space. Using liquid fuel under high pressure is a lot different from filling an ordinary gas tank.

The environmental systems are reviewed: how the air is kept fresh for breathing, how waste is disposed of, how the galley works.

The function of the communication and control systems is covered in detail. Pictures of electrical wiring circuits begin to appear in the individuals' sleep as well as on the classroom blackboard. Repetition is the order of the day. The candidates are becoming an expert repair crew, trained to cope with every imaginable emergency.

Orbital mechanics is on the agenda: how to control pitch, roll, and speed when flashing around the earth at 17,000 miles per hour with no brakes except a reverse thruster to slow the craft. Celestial navigation and space history are also studied.

The second part of the classroom work includes training in engineering, astronomy, geology, and the life sciences. Every one of these subjects could be a full university major. In some cases the critical information needed by an astronaut exceeds what is expected for a Ph.D. This is what is meant by being a generalist. This is the kind of person NASA searches for, a scientist who can expand his or her expertise to new fields.

Although the fleet of shuttles is always several hundred

miles from Houston, the astronauts receive hands-on training in sophisticated mock-ups at the Johnson Space Center. At the far end of the complex of buildings is a structure the size of a football field and several stories high. This is where the mock-ups are housed. Visitors are allowed in one section. The rest is off-limits unless you're scheduled for space flight in the near future.

At first glance it looks as if the shuttle mock-up has had a serious breakup in landing. The cockpit stands by itself on one side of the room, reached by a ladder. The cargo bay is held in place on a cradle in another area. Way at the back

Crews prepare for each flight a fully-equiped mission simulator at Houston. Sally Ride sits at the right in this picture.

you can see a kind of disjointed crane where the astronauts can practice retrieving satellites with the remote manipulator arm.

This is only one of the places where the astronaut candidates work at banks of controls simulating exact procedures in outer space, but it is the most complete. It is here that the classroom diagrams suddenly come to life. Everyone gets to stand in the cockpit of the craft and handle the controls. In emergencies, every crew member must be able to replace the pilot. They all have to learn each other's jobs.

Some of the astronauts are asked if there is any competition among them to see who can get the best grades. No, they say. "We just sort of compete with ourselves to absorb as much information as quickly as possible." Because it is so very important to a team of astronauts to be able to depend on each other in an emergency, there is a sense of camaraderie rather than competition, even in training.

However, some of the old-timers admit that just before flight assignments are about to be posted, there is a certain tension in the air. A chance to fly in space is the goal of every astronaut. After they've trained months for this opportunity, there's bound to be disappointment if they are passed by. Looking on the bright side, however, they realize that what one flight crew learns on a current mission makes the next flight safer for those who follow.

sixteen

Survival Training

*T*he class of '78 has to go through more training before they are ready for their turn in space. The most exciting, and the most frightening, training is yet to come. Orientation to flight training is next on the schedule.

The new class of astronauts starts by going up as back-seat drivers in Air Force T-38 jet planes. Even those pilots like Shannon Lucid, with several hundred hours of flight time, have never before experienced the "g" forces of such high-powered aircraft.

The T-38 is a two-seat trainer with dual controls. Instead of being intimidated, however, the new recruits are eager to take a turn as pilot. Permission is denied.

This jet trainer gives the astronauts a chance to learn the rear-seat procedures, to see the importance of having a second pair of eyes reporting on performance readings, and to handle comunication and flight planning.

They are also introduced to a larger plane, the K-135, affectionately called the "vomit comet." During training, the plane heads almost straight up toward the stratosphere. At the top of the ascent, it makes a sharp curve back toward the earth. It's a bit like being at the end of a crack-the-whip line. The maneuver picks their feet off the floor for 30 seconds of weightlessness. The inside of the cabin is padded to ease their fall back to the world of gravity.

"It's a little different," one of them remarks. Quite an understatement. But the first six women astronauts have no problems. Pictures show them grinning like kids on a roller coaster as they take swan dives and go "swimming in space."

Mary Cleave enjoys a few seconds of weightlessness aboard the K-135 training plane, also known as the "vomit comet."

Mary Cleave suspended in a parachute harness during survival training at Vance Air Force Base, Oklahoma.

Another first-year event is the Air Force Survival Course, which takes place at Homestead Air Force Base in Florida and at Vance Air Force Base near Enid, Oklahoma. "The purpose of the course is to prepare the trainees to eject from an aircraft, including the actual departure from the plane, the parachute drop, and subsequent survival measures over land or water."

It looks like fun, but there are a dozen sets of instructions to remember. Dressed in full flight gear, each astronaut candidate in turn is hooked to an open parachute. Then one at a time they are pulled off the deck of a stationary boat by a powerboat. Soon they are sailing 500 feet in the air above the water. A signal is given to drop the tow line. Before hitting the water they must struggle out of the harness, inflate the rubber raft they are carrying, and set off their rescue flares—not exactly the fun and games it had first appeared to be. But the candidates prove to be unflappable, and they gain the veterans' respect by showing that they can cut it.

Margaret Rhea Seddon takes part in the "drop and drag" phase of water survival training.

Bonnie Dunbar strapped into the ejection simulator during survival training at Vance Air Force Base, Oklahoma.

As soon as they finish the above-water tests, they are ready for the land training. For this part of their survival course, the candidates are flown to Oklahoma. First they are hung up in chute gear for short periods of time to get used to the feeling of being suspended in a parachute. Then they are attached to a parasail and pulled aloft by a pickup truck. This gives them the sensation of dropping from a high altitude. Sometimes these landings are harder than a fall from a plane. There are a few bruises, but no complaints.

There is also a diabolical gadget resembling a chair on rails. The astronauts line up in groups of ten. Each one has a turn at being strapped into the chair to wait for the countdown. At the signal the seat suddenly shoots straight up, as if the occupant were being blasted out of a plane in ejection gear.

The rest of the survival training is directly related to the shuttle. The only time the crew can evacuate the craft is on launch and during descent, shortly before a normal landing. There's always a possibility that something could go wrong with the firing mechanisms while the shuttle is still on the launchpad. If an abort is necessary before the solid rocket booster ignites, the access arm of the fixed service structure will move back into position so that the crew can exit through the hatch. Speed is important. Any emergency would probably involve the volatile firing mechanism of the shuttle, so there would be no time to take the elevator down.

The fastest way out of the shuttle is by way of slide wires. Five such wires extend from the service structure to the entrance of an underground bunker 1,200 feet away. There is a steel basket on each exit wire. Each basket holds two people. The entire crew can slide down the wires to the bunker in about thirty-five seconds—thirty-five seconds to safety.

A pad abort is possible any time before the solid boosters ignite, but once these have been fired, there's no immediate turning back; the shuttle is committed to at least a partial flight.

The most dangerous moment of a shuttle flight occurs during lift-off when the full force of the rocket boosters is pumping fuel into the main engine. It was at this moment that *Challenger* exploded on its ill-fated January, 1986, flight. There was no way that the shuttle could detach itself from its fiery tanks of fuel to set a course for an emergency landing.

Should an emergency arise after the shuttle is on its own, however, three landing sites are available. The closest one is at the Cape, within sight of the launch tower. With any altitude at all, however, considering the speed the shuttle attains from the booster rockets, the pilot could probably make an emergency landing at the U.S. Naval Air Station in Rota, Spain. Sophisticated communications systems are set up there and chase planes are on hand to guide a ship down. Edwards Air Force Base in California would be on the far range of the shuttle's path, but the craft could touch down there if necessary.

Science fiction writers have often dreamed up many nightmarish stories of astronauts being marooned in space. This is unlikely to happen with the shuttle. Normally both orbital maneuvering system engines fire for the slowdown and descent. If one fails, the other can function for the return. In the unlikely event that both are out of commission, there are still the weaker rockets that normally change the position of the shuttle outside the limits of gravity. These would have to be fired for a longer push to head the shuttle home, but computers, ground crews, and shuttle pilots practice these maneuvers just in case they ever need to use them.

If the worst happens and the shuttle remains in orbit in spite of all other efforts to return to the earth, there's the possibility of sending up another ship to bring the astronauts home. This of course was not possible when the class of '78 astronauts were in training, because the *Columbia* was the only shuttle in service at the time. But a fleet of four orbiters was eventually brought into service, so they were all put through the escape drills.

There are never more than two space suits aboard the shuttle. They are bulky and are used only for work outside the craft. In an emergency the crew would have to use rescue balls, those 30-inch fabric spheres that can be filled with enough oxygen to keep a person alive during the transfer from one space vehicle to another. The two astronauts assigned to wear the space suits would be responsible for attaching a line to the balls and delivering them to the rescue ship.

It is a frightening thought, but those astronauts who have passed the tests so far have proven themselves to have courage and faith in the safety of space flight. A lot can go wrong, but as scientists, the astronauts must consider the mathematical probabilities of an accident. Logically considering dangers ahead of time helps lessen panic if a malfunction should occur.

All have had the experience of being zipped into the tiny rescue balls. Anyone having an acute case of claustrophobia has been eliminated. It's a reassuring thought that such equipment has been provided.

There is one other time these "personal rescue enclosures" might be put to use. If a toxic gas should contaminate the air of the cabin, the crew could crawl into the balloons or don space suits while the shuttle is depressurized and the poison gas is vented.

Just in case they have to make an emergency or abnormal landing—caused, for example, by crippled landing gear—the candidates practice getting out of the shuttle as quickly as possible. Parachutes would be useless: the shuttle approaches land too fast and at too sharp an angle. The crew would have to exit after the craft landed on the ground.

When the hatch is open, a bar can be swung out to provide a handhold for jumping down to the ground. If the hatch sticks, a left-hand overhead window above the pilot's seat can be removed. Because the body of the shuttle would be extremely hot, an insulated panel would be unrolled over the side of the plane. A rope, such as a mountain climber uses to rappel down a cliff, is provided.

Safety precautions also include first aid training. Obviously, it would be ideal to have someone like Dr. Anna

Fisher, trained as an emergency medic, aboard each flight, but, even without her, every crew member is capable of treating injuries until the shuttle is back on Earth. The shuttle's medical kit includes everything from Band-Aids to a respirator and pills for various complaints.

One problem has affected some astronauts in the past. It is called space adaption syndrome, a tendency to feel nauseated in zero gravity. To treat this problem, a medicated patch can be attached behind the ear of an astronaut. The medicine is absorbed slowly through the skin to halt the symptoms of nausea without decreasing the alertness of the astronaut. Before heading for space, the astronauts are tested for certain doses. It isn't helpful to have a sleepy mission specialist fumbling with experiments. Their responses are monitored at all times.

seventeen

Suiting Up

*A*fter the rugged orientation program is over, more specific jobs are assigned. Anna Fisher is surprised to find herself under water for the first few months—not every hour of the day, but enough to make her wonder if she's being trained to explore the sea bottom rather than outer space.

Actually the tank she is in has been carefully designed to fake the conditions an astronaut will feel in zero gravity. It is possible, with just the right balance of weight and buoyancy, to glide around in the water as you would in space. True, water acts as a slight drag. There will be none in space, but this feeling is as close to weightlessness as is possible on earth.

Anna has already passed tests as a scuba diver, but this didn't prepare her for the work she is expected to do in a bulky diving suit. The suit is much like the extravehicular mobility unit garment meant for space walks. Even the helmet and backpack are designed to give the diver the same angle of vision, mobility, and balance that he or she will have in outer space.

The big neutral buoyancy simulator tank is located at the Marshall Space Center in Huntsville, Alabama. It is 75 feet wide and 50 feet deep, filled with 1.3 million gallons of clear water. A smaller tank is located at the Johnson Center. Anna is scheduled to test how well a person can use specific tools in water and in space.

Already in place at the bottom of the tank is a mock-up of a space platform with a solar array system, which in space would be the battery pack energized by the sun. Anna is given a dry run of just what she's expected to do: remove the whole pack, all 900 pounds of it, which in water or space weighs nothing.

This involves opening a pair of latches, removing a set of slide pins, and reassembling the pieces. When that is done, she is to head for the "phone booth," a boxed section with mock electric boxes. There she must make connections on seven wires of different thicknesses.

Another astronaut in space gear is in the water with Anna, and two scuba divers are there in case either astronaut gets tangled in the equipment.

It takes a bit of doing just to get into the diving gear. Anna starts by putting on pants, then bending over to dive into the top and cram her head through the neck ring. Inside the suit, straps have been tightened to adjust the fit to her smaller size. Still, she looks like a small hippo with pleated knees.

She carefully backs into a boxlike cradle with forward-jutting arms. In a moment a crane lifts the whole apparatus high in the air, then gently lowers it into the tank. Clear water swirls over her face plate while television cameras record every movement.

A complete life-support system takes care of Anna's air

supply, and she can communicate with her partner and with the "ground crew." A metal rack across the chest plate of her suit gives her a place to hang tools that might float out of her reach.

The gloves she wears were made as flexible as possible after months of research, but they are still clumsy. The first thing she must do is find a foot- or handhold to keep herself in position for her job and to prevent her from floating away, a problem astronauts have had in space.

"If you can do it in the water tank, you can do it in zero gravity," said Jack Lousma, commander of the second Skylab crew. "It's a great training and development tool." When Lousma was up in space, he beamed down the enthusiastic message, "It's just like the tank in Huntsville, only deeper."

Anna continues to work slowly, patiently. It is tiring work. At the end of two hours she is ready to be hoisted to the surface again.

Both astronauts are questioned on how the job can be made easier. Could tools be improved? Should extra handholds be added to the equipment? Every comment is noted, and then it's back to the tank for another exercise.

The outfit for space walks is a close copy of the tank suit. It is a monstrously heavy garment on Earth when attached to the portable life-support system backpack. Yet it is a great improvement over the less flexible model that Edward H. White wore in 1965 on America's first space walk.

Beneath the suit the astronaut wears a cooling and ventilation garment made of spandex mesh with plastic tubing woven into it. With the extremes of hot and cold in outer space, this is a lifesaving part of the suit.

The space suit, known as the extravehicular mobility unit, or EMU, is made in several standard sizes. Inside the

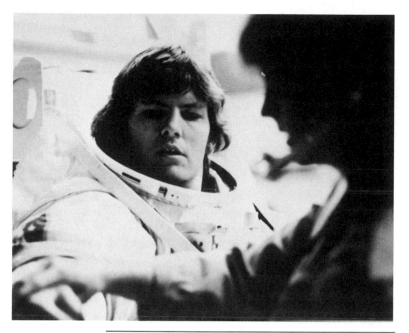

Kathryn Sullivan being prepared for a rehearsal of her spacewalk at the weightless environment training facility at the Johnson Space Center.

suit are straps that can be adjusted for an acceptable fit. The EMU is made in three parts. The upper torso, or chest, portion is rigid with aluminum supports. A chest-mounted microcomputer tells the astronaut how much oxygen and battery power he or she has left. Other instruments are mounted here, too. With the push of a button the wearer can control temperature, fan, radio, and rate of oxygen intake.

Trousers come with boots attached. A connecting ring around the waist joins the two parts. Shoulder, elbow, and knee joints resemble a pleated bellows, so that as one side contracts the other expands, keeping the interior volume, and hence the pressure, constant.

Gloves are made in fifteen different sizes. They have molded finger caps so that the wearer has a certain amount of feeling for delicate jobs.

The helmet is similar to that worn by the astronauts who landed on the moon. Inside the plastic bubble helmet are two microphones and a set of earphones. A gold-plated visor protects the eyes from ultraviolet radiation and from micrometeoroids.

The old suits took more than an hour to put on, and a "dresser" was required to check zip locks and hose connections. With the new design, a space walker can dress and undress in a matter of minutes. However, preparation starts at least two hours before the exit into space. The reason for this is that the cabin atmosphere of the shuttle is 79 percent nitrogen and 21 percent oxygen and is kept constantly at a slightly higher pressure than is used inside the suit. A crew member would suffer from the bends if he or she were to go directly into the pure oxygen pressure-reduced environment of the space suit. The nitrogen gas dissolved in the blood would bubble out, causing painful pressure around the joints.

About two hours before dressing for space, astronauts start breathing pure oxygen from a face mask. This slowly "washes" the nitrogen from their bodies.

Space workers who are ready to leave the ship must travel through an airlock to avoid depressurizing the entire crew compartment.

For some work in space a power unit, or manned maneuvering unit (MMU), is added to the backpack. It looks a lot like the cradle Anna Fisher used in the water tank. The arms that jut forward hold the controls. Twenty-four jets powered by pressurized nitrogen are capable of accelerating to speeds of 66 feet (19 meters) per second. However, for most tasks, the astronauts use much slower movements—about the speed you'd be going up an escalator.

Yet these figures are all relative, as the free-flying astronauts are already traveling at 17,500 miles per hour as they circle the earth once every 90 minutes. There is no sensation of speed, however. It is as if they were drifting weightlessly in the water tank at Huntsville.

That may seem strange, but think of a fly inside a car that is going 50 miles an hour. It can't really be said the fly itself is traveling at that speed, yet it travels that far.

These MMUs were first used in February 1984 by astronauts Bruce McCandless and Robert Stewart. It was the first time a human, without being attached by tether to a spaceship, had become a satellite himself.

Every astronaut practices the procedures for work outside the shuttle, even if the mission will not require such a procedure. It's a kind of lifeboat drill.

eighteen

Where They Hang the Bird

While Anna Fisher was floating in the neutral buoyancy tank, Judy Resnik and Sally Ride were working in Toronto, Canada, with the engineers of SPAR Aerospace Ltd. It was here the scientists developed the remote manipulator system, or RMS, which Sally Ride and John Fabian later used to retrieve a piece of equipment on the STS-7 flight.

They practiced until they were able to pick up small, delicate instruments as well as large, cumbersome objects. "It got to be as natural as using tweezers on a noodle," Sally laughs. "I began to think that all there was to being an astronaut was launching an arm."

Everybody was doing her own thing. Shannon Lucid spent time in California working on landing procedures. Kathy Sullivan worked on computer calculations for alternative landing sites. Training increasingly became a matter of self-discipline.

"Your job description is generally a one-liner," Kathy Sullivan said. " 'Why don't you go work at the Cape?' Nobody sits on you to make sure you work from eight to four. It's 'Get the job done.' "

You do it, they all say, because you are continually challenged, continually learning—something that is very important to these extraordinary people.

Every one of the astronauts is expected to keep up with his or her own specialty. That may mean continuing research through a university or spending hours studying technical papers published by others.

To sharpen their medical skills both Anna and Rhea rode in rescue helicopters. "In training exercises," Dr. Seddon says, "we try to simulate situations that could actually happen. We 'rescue' uniformed dummies, perform emergency procedures on them in shaky, noisy helicopters, and then get them to our backup trauma centers." The astronauts were being trained to give emergency care at launchings and landings.

By the time Bonnie Dunbar and Mary Cleave reached Houston in 1980, women had become familiar members of the astronaut corps. Both women came into the program with specialties of their own. Mary Cleave was a sanitary engineer with excellent credentials from her work with micro-organisms, looking toward the future when a closed-loop recycle system would be a necessity in a space station. Her first job was to work on the space toilet of the shuttle.

"Right now I'm working at SAIL, the Shuttle Avionics Integration Lab," she explains. "The lab runs twenty-four hours a day, seven days a week. One week I could go to work at seven in the morning and get off about four or five. The next week I could get the swing shift or the graveyard shift, just like any factory worker. On my last shift, I was testing ascent procedures."

Bonnie Dunbar was already well acquainted with NASA, having been in on the beginning of the heat shield testing for the shuttle. She had gotten used to some pretty incredible facts and figures about space travel, but big surprises awaited her at the Cape. That is were tiny mortals control giant machines, where they "hang the bird," fuel it, test cargo packages, and put it all together.

Approached from the west, Cape Canaveral is a desolate-looking landscape at first glance, water-pocked swampland and palmetto brush. Yet the space center, which is surrounded by the Merritt Island National Wildlife Refuge, covering 140,000 acres of land and water, protects more endangered species of birds, mammals, and reptiles than any other area of the continental United States. Just don't step too far off the cleared tracks, because this wildlife also includes several kinds of poisonous snakes. Somehow, life seems to have sorted itself out satisfactorily. The public comes to look only; the staff of the military and space complex comes to work; the wildlife is there to make its home, and each has laid out privacy markers of its own.

The string-straight horizon is broken by the imposing fifty-story Vehicle Assembly Building and by the towering scaffolds of the launch pads. The headquarters of the Kennedy Space Center is a long factory-like building that houses the management offices and several thousand contracted and support personnel. All together, some thirteen thousand people are employed in the complex, making it a small city in itself.

The Central Instrumentation Facility is filled with space-age computers. Its huge dish-shaped radio antenna forms the satellite communications link between the Kennedy Space Center, Mission Control in Houston, and other NASA centers.

The giant 525-foot, 8-acre Vehicle Assembly Building at the Kennedy Space Center.

In the Flight Crew Training Building simulated problems can be fed into computers. It is here also that the parachutes for the fuel tanks are cleaned, inspected, and repackaged.

The Orbiter Processing Facility is essentially a hangar with two high bays in which orbiters, two at a time, can undergo servicing after landing. It is here that propellant feedlines are drained and cleaned, flight and landing systems are refurbished, returned payloads are removed, and everything is set in motion for the next mission.

Dominating the entire landscape is the 525-foot-tall Vehicle Assembly Building, which covers eight acres of ground. With an inside volume of 129 million cubic feet, it is one of the world's largest enclosed structures. Under certain conditions, it develops weather all its own. Changing climate can cause updrafts and even an occasional fog bank to form inside the building, something to guard against.

When the orbiter is ready for processing, it is towed through the towering doors. Huge cranes hoist it into a vertical position, lift it 190 feet above the floor, then swing it gently over a large structural beam and lower it to the deck of the mobile launch platform.

The twin solid-rocket boosters are erected on the platform first; the fifteen-story external belly tank is added. Here the whole shuttle is assembled while standing on its tail.

The next task is to move the unwieldy shuttle three and a half miles away to the launch pad. This job is done by a crawler transporter, a huge vehicle capable of lifting and carrying 14,500,000 pounds. Each transporter is about half the size of a soccer field and weighs about 6 million pounds. Two diesel generators drive the electric motors that turn the huge tank-like tread on the transporter. Each

A fully-prepared shuttle is moved slowly to the launch pad at the Kennedy Space Center.

cleat of the crawler weighs a ton. A special runway had to be constructed that would withstand the tremendous weight of these vehicles without caving in or buckling.

A hydraulic system can raise, lower, or tilt the transporter so that the shuttle remains level as it is moved up the incline to the launch pad. One man does the driving, but twenty-six other engineers are also aboard to check every procedure along the way. When the vehicle is loaded, its speed is only about one mile an hour.

Bonnie visits the area several times to watch these exciting steps. She also inspects the shuttles for burn damage before they are reserviced.

She looks longingly at the spacecraft. "I'm not trying to overcompensate for being a woman," Dunbar insists, "but with enough flying time, who knows? One of us could get to command a mission sometime. Then we'll get our chance to fly that beautiful shuttle."

nineteen

Whose Turn Next?

What do these superpowered women do in their down-to-earth time off? Just about the same things their neighbors do. All of them enjoy sports. For some, it is an activity they've always enjoyed. Others have taken up sports more recently to keep in shape.

The Fishers are likely to go backpacking in a remote spot on their days off. Kathy Sullivan loves to sail, and she's proved herself a winning skipper. But at the moment she's without a boat of her own—not enough time for one. Mary Cleave goes back to Utah every now and then to visit the old gang and do some skiing, but she finds it hard to play the role of celebrity.

"[Fame] has its disadvantages," she says. She was in a grocery store one day when she noticed that the other shoppers were staring. "First they'd ask me if they hadn't seen my picture. Was I an astronaut? Then they'd start looking over every single thing in my shopping cart. They'd ask me why I was buying junk food. You just can't be perfect."

119

There's an occasional backyard barbecue in the Houston area when a NASA group gets together. Sally Ride met her husband Steven Hawley in 1978 while they were both in training for the space program. Steven is a graduate of the University of California where he earned a Ph.D. in astronomy, which is Sally's field of interest, too. They were married July 24, 1982. The bride wore Levis and a Rugby shirt and flew her own plane to the wedding in her husband's hometown in Kansas.

Rhea Seddon and Anna Fisher have chosen to combine motherhood and space travel. Rhea married astronaut pilot Lieutenant Commander Robert Gibson. Their son, Paul Seddon Gibson, was born in 1982, and the Fishers' daughter, Kirstin Ann, arrived a year later. Shannon Lucid's kids were already of school age when she became an astronaut.

Each of the women has been given plenty of responsibility. Sally Ride, for example, was destined to do more than work with the remote manipulator system. She also served as a capcom, or capsule communicator, the earth-based link between the astronauts in space and the people on the ground, what TV commentators have called "the voice of Mission Control." In November 1981, during the second shuttle flight, it was Sally who broke the news to astronauts Joe Engle and Dick Truly that their mission had to be cut short because of the loss of a power-producing cell.

During the third shuttle flight Ride again was the capcom at Mission Control when the robot arm was being tested. A broken camera on the arm threatened to cancel the experiment. She came up with a solution to the problem, which salvaged that portion of the work.

On that same flight the astronauts were taking blood samples of each other and analyzing them. Suddenly one of the astronauts appeared on the television screen hanging upside down from *Columbia's* ceiling. Abandoning her

Sally Ride at the mission control center in Houston, where she will talk with astronauts during the STS-2 flight as they work with the remote manipulator system.

businesslike communications style, Ride radioed, "Hey, is that the vampire to go with the red blood cells?"

Rumors had been spreading that one of the eight women would soon be scheduled for a flight. It's been said that the biggest mystery around is how flight crews are chosen, although it is assumed that George Abbey, director of flight operations, and John Young, chief of the astronaut office and commander of the first shuttle flight, make the final decision.

Abbey, who wears his military crew cut at practically scalp level, has the unenviable task of selecting each flight commander. The commander, in turn, makes suggestions about the choice of crew members.

The idea is to find the most experienced person for the job at hand. When the announcement was made that Sally Ride was to be the first women from the United States in space, this qualifying statement was also issued: "Since the women are there because of their skills, Dr. Ride's selection for STS-7 doesn't imply that she is the best of the women astronauts. Her skills were most needed on this particular mission."

Commander Robert Crippen gave his reasons for seconding Sally's selection. "Sally is a very smart lady. She is smart in a special way. You get people who sit in the lab and think like Einstein, but they can't do anything with it. Now, Sally can get everything she knows together and bring it to bear where you need it. . . . There's an awful lot to watch up there, and we need a third pair of eyeballs."

"Any one of us would like to swap places with Sally," Kathy Sullivan said after the announcement was made. "And yet being first brings with it an added load of responsibility. I don't know that any one of us can ever put all the skeptics to rest, and it's unfair that Sally should have that burden entirely on her shoulders."

"Sally was selected for this flight as testimony to her ability to perform on the job," said Mary Cleave. "She's going to blow everyone's socks off, because she's a real competent lady. There will be a bunch of little girls on this planet who will be looking at Sally and saying, 'Hey, if I want to be an astrophysicist, that's okay.' It gives girls of today options we didn't have when we were kids."

Sally Ride followed her historic first flight with a second, in the Fall of 1984. She was also to become involved in the space program in other important ways. After the explosion which destroyed the shuttle Challenger in January, 1986,

Sally was made a member of the Presidential inquiry investigating the accident. Her most recent job at NASA has been as a special assistant to the director of long-range planning, where she has been working on a report on the space agency's objectives for the future.

It was therefore quite a surprise when she announced, in May, 1987, that she would be leaving the astronaut corps to return to Stanford University. She will be studying arms control and national security. In a statement, she said: "The various projects I have participated in have provided unique challenges and have allowed me to grow as a scientist and a person. It is in that same spirit of challenge that I have accepted the post at Stanford University." Dr. James Fletcher, Administrator of NASA, said that "Her flight . . . firmly established an equal role for women in the space exploration program."

Sally Ride has her own page in history, but there is

Kathryn Sullivan uses a pair of binoculars to look down at the Earth's surface from her position in orbit aboard the *Challenger.*

plenty more to put on the record. The original six women astronauts and the two who were chosen later have all flown on shuttle missions.

Judy Resnik's first flight took place between August 30 and September 5, 1984. On the following mission, October 5 to October 13, 1984, two women were aboard: Sally Ride and Kathy Sullivan, who became the first women to walk in space.

Anna Fisher had her chance November 8–16, 1985, and Rhea Seddon January 24–27, 1985. Shannon Lucid patiently waited for her turn until June 17–24, 1985. Bonnie Dunbar was on the flight that took place October 30–November 6, 1985. Right behind her came Mary Cleave, November 26–December 3, 1985.

In the meantime NASA had announced the selection of other astronaut candidates to fill their ranks with extraordinary talent. Five more women will be taking their place on the pages of space records.

Marsha Ivins of Baltimore, Maryland, received her aerospace engineering degree from the University of Colorado.

Tamara Jernigan, one of the youngest candidates, was born May 7, 1959. Her specialty is astronomy.

Linda Godwin has a Ph.D. in physics, as does Kathryn Thornton of Montgomery, Alabama. Ellen Baker is a medical doctor.

But what caught the imagination of the public was the selection of an "ordinary person," without any training in space flight or science, as a "space participant" on a shuttle mission. In August 1984, when President Reagan was running for his second term of office, he announced that he wanted a teacher to be the first citizen observer in space.

The aim, of course, was to build broad public support and confidence in the space program. Most of us have never met an astronaut, but we all know teachers. If a

Christa McAuliffe, the teacher chosen by NASA to become the first "ordinary person" in space. She was killed when the shuttle *Challenger* exploded on January 28, 1986.

teacher could travel in space, the future would seem to be open for all of us to follow.

More than 11,000 teachers applied for the chance to fly in the shuttle. Christa McAuliffe was chosen. Her talents lay not in her scientific expertise but in her ability to project enthusiasm for her job, which made her an excellent public relations person. McAuliffe's job was to conduct two fifteen-minute classes in space for millions of earthbound schoolchildren who would be watching the flight on closed-circuit television. She would conduct a tour of the spacecraft and explain the duties of each crew member and the facilities on board.

In her second lesson Christa McAuliffe would try to answer these questions: Where have we been? Where are we going? Why are we doing this? The lesson would include the scientific, commercial, and industrial benefits to be gained from space travel—a tall order to cover in a short time.

Flight 51-L carried a $100 million NASA satellite and instruments that would measure the ultraviolet spectrum of Halley's Comet. Other gauges would sample radiation aboard the spacecraft at various stages in orbit. The shuttle also carried a student project whose aim was to study the effect of weightlessness on the development of chicken embryos.

The shuttle crew included Flight Commander Francis R. Scobee, Pilot Michael J. Smith, Ronald E. McNair, Ellison S. Onizuka, Gregory B. Jarvis, and Judith Resnik. They were an remarkably diversified group: male, female; black, white, Japanese-American; Catholic, Jewish, and Protestant.

The *Challenger*'s tenth journey was scheduled for lift-off on January 20, 1986, but dust storms at an emergency landing facility delayed the launch for twenty-four hours. Another delay was caused by a sticky bolt that prevented the removal of an outside latch handle. By the time this minor problem was solved, the weather had worsened, with gusts of wind up to 35 mph that would have made an emergency landing at the Cape too dangerous.

On the night of January 27 the temperature at the Florida launch site had dropped to an unseasonable 27 degrees, but skies were clearing and winds were normal. The crew was ready. The countdown resumed.

At T minus seven minutes thirty seconds the walkway was pulled away from *Challenger*. At T minus two minutes and twenty seconds the shuttle was operating on its own electrical power. All systems seemed to be normal.

Finally the moment came when in a burst of power the rockets lifted the spaceship off its pad in a slow, graceful arc that trailed a scallop of smoke across the blue sky. Cheers came from a thousand spectators watching from bleachers some four miles from Pad 39-B.

But then, just seventy-three seconds after lift-off, the trail burst into streaks of orange, yellow, and red, giving birth to a jagged white cloud that snaked wildly out of control as the shuttle headed for the ocean nine miles below, disintegrating as it fell.

The nation watched in shocked horror. There were those who had spoken of the dangers of space flight, but the public had become complacent. Americans had soared into space fifty-five times over twenty-five years. There had been twenty-four successful shuttle launches. The astronauts' safe return was taken for granted. People forgot that the space shuttle was the most complex flying machine ever built, much more intricate than the rocket that had carried men to the moon.

The world mourned. Soviet officials announced that they were naming two newly discovered craters on the planet Venus in honor of Resnik and McAuliffe. Only the women were chosen, they explained, because Venus was named for a Roman goddess.

All over the United States flags flew at half-mast. Memorial services were held for the crew. The President said, "They wished to serve, and they did. They served all of us."

One question was paramount: How did it happen? Again and again pictures of the mishap were shown on screens and analyzed by NASA scientists. A flickering glow just past the center of the shuttle's belly and the right external booster tank flared seconds before the fatal explosion.

There was hope that some of the debris salvaged from the ocean would hold the answer. Thirteen aircraft and more than a dozen recovery vessels covered 6,000 square miles of water. There were still missing parts to the puzzle. NASA knew that unless they could come up with the answers, there would be a long and perhaps permanent delay in future space exploration. A committee was appointed by Congress to sift through the evidence.

The most widely accepted explanation for the accident was that a seal at the joint of the external tank had been defective. Had the cold weather caused the malfunction? Everyone agreed that there had been too little margin of safety. Obviously the booster rockets and ring seals would have to be redesigned before any other flights would be scheduled.

This meant that the ambitious calendar for launches in 1986 had to be scrubbed. Many important scientific experiments would not be carried aloft by the shuttle in the near future. The military had priority over projects with long-range goals.

President Reagan tried to quiet rumors that the shuttle program itself would be canceled. Too much time and money had already been invested to scrap it, but some critics felt that too much confidence had been placed in one system, ignoring the possibility that unmanned rockets could send satellites into orbit at a lower cost with no human risk.

It's too late to turn the clock back now, and few would want to. We are committed to putting men and women into an environment where they can further explore the wonders of the universe. There is still an exciting project ahead: a permanent space station in orbit, a commuter stop for more specialized vehicles heading for distant destinations.

Women will play a part in these explorations. The original women astronauts have proved that sex is no restriction to talent and courage. The world is waiting for knowledge that can only come from an environment beyond the boundaries of the Earth's gravity and the blurring effect of our atmosphere. There are bound to be exciting discoveries ahead.

SUGGESTED FURTHER READINGS

Bendick, Jeanne. *Space Travel*. New York: Franklin Watts, 1982.
Berger, Melvin. *Space Shots, Shuttles and Satellites*. New York: Putnam, 1983.
Hodgman, Ann, and Ruby Djabbaroff. *Skystars: The History of Women in Aviation*. New York: Atheneum, 1981.
O'Connor, Karen. *Sally Ride and the New Astronauts*. New York: Franklin Watts, 1983.
Pastor, Terry, illus. *Space Mission*. Boston: Little, Brown, 1983.
Smith, Elizabeth Simpson. *Breakthrough: Women in Aviation*. New York: Walker, 1981.
Vogt, Gregory. *The Space Shuttle: Projects for Young Scientists*. New York: Franklin Watts, 1983.

INDEX

131

ABOUT THE AUTHOR

Mary Virginia Fox was born in Richmond, Virginia. She graduated from Northwestern University, as did her entire family for the past three generations. She is the author of many books for young people. She lives with her husband and three sons in Middleton, Wisconsin, and spends most of her time writing and traveling.